ON ENVIRONMENTAL GOVERNANCE

ON POLITICS

L. Sandy Maisel, Series Editor

On Politics is a new series of short reflections by major scholars on key subfields within political science. Books in the series are personal and practical as well as informed by years of scholarship and deliberation. General readers who want a considered overview of a field as well as students who need a launching platform for new research will find these books a good place to start. Designed for personal libraries as well as student backpacks, these smart books are small format, easy reading, aesthetically pleasing, and affordable.

Titles in the Series

ORAN R. YOUNG

ON ENVIRONMENTAL GOVERNANCE

Sustainability, Efficiency, and Equity

Routledge
Taylor & Francis Group

LONDON AND NEW YORK

First published 2013 by Paradigm Publishers

Published 2016 by Routledge
2 Park Square, Milton Park, Abingdon, Oxon OX14 4RN
711 Third Avenue, New York, NY 10017, USA

Routledge is an imprint of the Taylor & Francis Group, an informa business

Library of Congress Cataloging-in-Publication Data

Young, Oran R.
    On environmental governance : sustainability, efficiency, and equity / Oran
R. Young.
        p. cm. — (On Politics)
    Includes bibliographical references and index.
    ISBN 978-1-61205-132-1 (hardcover : alk. paper) — ISBN 978-1-61205-
133-8 (pbk. : alk. paper)
    1. Environmental policy. 2. Environmental protection. 3. Sustainability.
4. Environmental justice. I. Title.
GE170.Y683 2012
333.7—dc23   2012003114

ISBN 13: 978-1-61205-132-1 (hbk)
ISBN 13: 978-1-61205-133-8 (pbk)

To our children and grandchildren,
who will confront the environmental
challenges of 2050

Contents

FIGURES

PREFACE

When Jennifer Knerr approached me with the idea of writing *On Environmental Governance* as a volume in Paradigm's *On Politics* series, my first reaction was one of skepticism. Although I have transitioned from active teaching status to emeritus/research professor status, I find that I am just as busy as ever. My latest theoretical work is appearing in places like the *Proceedings of the National Academy of Sciences* and the *International Studies Review*. The areas I focus on in my applied work—climate, the oceans, the polar regions—are all hot topics in policy circles at this time. I am fortunate enough to have opportunities to communicate my thoughts about matters of governance arising in these areas to a variety of audiences on a regular basis. I am engaged in active collaborative efforts with colleagues in places as far apart as China and Iceland. So I thought to myself that there simply is not room to fit a project like this book into my schedule.

On reflection, however, I realized that I needed to revise my priorities. This project would offer an excellent opportunity to lay out the main lines of my thinking about environmental governance as they have developed over the last forty years and present them in a form that any interested reader could absorb without making a major investment of time. This point was brought home to me in a conversation with my adult daughter, who has a lively interest in environmental governance but is not in a position to invest a large chunk of time in reading a longer and more academic book on this topic. She observed, "I'm really curious about environmental governance, and of course, I'd like to have a better understanding of what you do. But my life is so busy that I have limited time to read, much less give a more formal, academic work the focus and time it requires. *On Environmental Governance* sounds like exactly the sort of book I'd really enjoy." My guess is that many will share her reaction. No doubt, a sizable proportion of those who read this book will be students who encounter it as a reading assignment on a course syllabus—that is all to the good. But I am particularly excited by the prospect that the readership for this book may extend to members of a larger reading public who are aware that there are complex and important governance questions relating to areas like climate change, the oceans, and the polar regions but have neither the time nor the background to plunge into the more formal literature in this field. This book is for them!

For these readers I should emphasize that the book is not about providing simple answers. You will not find here neatly packaged recommendations about how to break the impasse in efforts to strengthen the climate regime or whether to push toward negotiating a legally binding treaty for the Arctic. Rather, my objective is to provide a coherent framework for thinking about such matters and to develop a mode of analysis that can yield concrete recommendations regarding specific issues arising in specific places at specific times. The key to the process lies in what I call institutional diagnostics. Just as we would expect an architect to design a building well suited to relevant biophysical conditions, economic circumstances, and intended uses, we should expect those seeking to design governance systems to recommend arrangements that fit well with all the pertinent biophysical and socioeconomic conditions. There is no reason to assume, for instance, that what worked when dealing with the depletion of stratospheric ozone will solve the climate problem or that what worked in addressing the challenges of the Antarctic will work in the Arctic. But the practice of institutional diagnostics can draw on lessons derived from experience with other cases in the process of developing plans that have a reasonable prospect of proving successful in current situations.

As I explain in the body of the book, there is a growing urgency about improving our ability to address challenges of environmental governance. Increasingly, we inhabit a human-dominated planet where the activities of human beings collectively are responsible for major changes on the Earth on a planetary scale. The problem of climate change is only the most prominent example of a growing class of challenges of this sort. For our own sake as well as for the well-being of the Earth's other inhabitants we must find ways to govern human behavior so as to avoid the destructive consequences of our actions without sacrificing social welfare. For anyone who expects to be alive in 2030 to 2050, this is likely to become an overriding concern.

I am grateful to a large circle of friends and colleagues with whom I have had the privilege of discussing these issues over many years. Of course, I take responsibility for any errors or other shortcomings to be found in the text of the book. But much of my thinking about environmental governance bears the marks of long-standing and ongoing dialogues with others who think about such matters in many parts of the globe.

INTRODUCTION
GOVERNING HUMAN-ENVIRONMENT
RELATIONS

Humans use natural resources and interact with the environment sustainably in some settings but not in others. Some groups are able to harvest fish on a basis that is sustainable over time, whereas others deplete stocks rapidly. Some groups enjoy clean air and clear water, whereas others suffer from severe pollution produced as a side effect of industrial activities. What explains these differences in the outcomes arising from human-environment relations? Those seeking answers to this question have pointed to a variety of factors, including population, affluence, and technology. But what stands out in every case is the role of governance. Where effective governance systems are in place, humans can interact with nature in such a way as to avoid problems like land degradation, the depletion of fish stocks, and climate change. Where such systems are underdeveloped or dysfunctional, the costs both to individuals and to society at large can become severe. In today's globalized world these costs can range all the way from the impacts of air pollution on the health of single individuals to the impacts of rising atmospheric concentrations of greenhouse gases on the planet's climate system.

Broadly speaking, environmental governance becomes a matter of public concern when human actions—individually or collectively—threaten the sustainability of ecosystems, degrade ecosystem services, generate side effects impacting human well-being, or violate societal standards regarding efficiency, equity, and good governance in the use of natural resources. From this vantage point it is easy to see that phrases like environmental management or ecosystem management are misleading. What we can aspire to manage or, more generally, govern are human actions. The resultant efforts may include the development of social practices guiding human uses of natural resources, the launching of initiatives aimed at bolstering the resilience of ecosystem services, and the conduct of research undertaken to enhance understanding of socioecological systems for the purpose of promoting informed choices on the part of human users. But none of this alters the fact that environmental governance is a matter of guiding or steering the behavior of human actors in the interests of avoiding socially undesirable outcomes (e.g., the tragedy of the commons) and enhancing the achievement of socially desirable ends (e.g., the conservation of ecosystem services). It follows that we need to bring the knowledge and the research methods of the social sciences to bear not only to enhance our understanding of environmental governance but also to expand our capacity to create and administer the governance systems needed to achieve desired ends in the realm of human-environment relations.

In those (increasingly rare) situations in which human actors lack the capacity to affect biophysical systems significantly or supplies of resources are plentiful enough to satisfy the needs or wants of all human users, we can do without governance systems. Put another way, arrangements that do not impose prohibitions or requirements on the behavior of users are appropriate in such cases. Relying on such arrangements does not lead to socially undesirable outcomes, and these practices avoid the costs associated with creating and implementing regulatory systems. As soon as human actions become significant drivers in socioecological systems, however, the need to establish governance arrangements that can address issues of sustainability as well as efficiency and equity does arise. As we move deeper into an era characterized by human domination of biophysical systems from the local level on up to the global level, the need to create effective systems of environmental governance is rising rapidly.[1] Some observers hold out the hope that the necessary arrangements will arise spontaneously or in the absence of deliberate actions in the form of informal social conventions or norms, thereby eliminating the need for conscious efforts to create effective systems to govern human-environment relations. However governance systems arise, many users of natural resources and ecosystem services react antagonistically to the impacts of the resultant restrictions on their freedom of action. But there is no escaping the fact that rising human pressures on biophysical systems have generated a sharp rise in the need for governance on a global scale. The challenge before us is to devise innovative arrangements to channel human actions in the interests of achieving sustainability while minimizing the imposition of limitations on the freedom of human actors to use natural resources and ecosystem services for their own ends.

My goal in this short book is to examine a range of efforts to meet this challenge and to explore new options for governing human-environment relations that may prove effective under the conditions prevailing in a human-dominated world.[2] I will draw on a number of more general ideas about the nature of governance, the need for governance in various settings, and the operation of governance systems in addressing this challenge. I hope to demonstrate as well that an analysis of governance focused on environmental issues can contribute to our understanding of governance more generally. In practical terms my goal is to provide a toolkit with which to tackle specific issues of environmental governance rather than simply provide answers to questions ranging from how to harvest fish sustainably to how to avoid the problem of climate change.

Governance

At the most general level governance is a social function centered on efforts to steer or guide the actions of human groups—from small, local associations to international society—toward the achievement of desired ends and away from outcomes regarded as undesirable.[3] Although humans have devised a variety of means to perform this function, the need for governance is common to all social groups, and governance systems can and often do address a variety of concerns ranging from issues arising in interactions among owners of property to the maintenance of public health and the protection of the group in the face of external threats to individual members or the group as a whole. In simple situations where the actions of individual group members have little or no impact on the well-being of others and there are no external threats to the welfare of the group, minimal forms of governance are all that are needed to achieve desired ends. Open-to-entry systems that impose few restrictions on the actions of individual users of renewable resources exemplify this pattern. As the size of the group increases and the impacts of the activities of individual members grow, however, the need for governance rises. In large, modern societies the need for governance emerges as a critical societal concern. To use the previous example, complex restrictions on the actions of harvesters of renewable resources are essential in such settings as a means to ensure sustainability, much less efficiency and equity. Guiding the actions of human actors, both individually and collectively, has come into focus as one of the overriding challenges of our era.

Is Government Necessary?

Given this conception of governance it is easy to show that the presence of a government in the normal sense of the term is neither sufficient nor necessary to succeed in performing the function of governance. A number of factors can suppress or derail actions on the part of governments to fulfill needs for governance. Governments may be poorly informed regarding the relevant issues, afflicted with institutional arthritis attributable to the growth of unwieldy bureaucracies, or crippled by political deadlocks that sap their ability to govern effectively. Corruption in high places frequently produces governments more oriented toward promoting the ends of a few powerful individuals than toward addressing needs for governance. In extreme cases governments become instruments of oppression or persecution rather than mechanisms dedicated to steering human interactions toward desired ends. Whatever vision we have of the ideal of good governance, then, there is no basis for assuming that actual governments will play effective roles in addressing needs for governance.

Arguably of greater interest in this exploration of environmental governance is the observation that the existence of a government in the normal sense is not necessary to meet the needs for governance in a variety of settings.[4] There are cases in which processes for addressing needs for governance arise spontaneously or at least in the absence of a public authority designated as the body responsible for dealing with matters of governance. Although the leading examples of what has become known as governance without government involve small-scale social systems held together by a strong sense of community, this phenomenon occurs at other levels as well. A prominent example is the international regime that has developed since the 1980s to deal with the depletion of stratospheric ozone by phasing out the production and consumptions of ozone-depleting substances like chlorofluorocarbons and halons.[5] There are also cases in which actors other than governments (often labeled nonstate actors in the political science literature) take on responsibility for performing the function of governance. This has given rise to a lively interest in the potential of private governance as well as in the emergence of various hybrid arrangements involving governance on the part of some combination of public agencies, private actors, and entities rooted in civil society.[6] The conditions under which governance without government becomes a realistic option are not yet well understood, but the prospect that societies can come to terms with needs for governance without relying entirely on the actions of governments is a source of hope, particularly for those concerned with global issues like climate change.

Governance as a Social Enterprise

Governance systems are arrangements that social groups develop, either spontaneously or through deliberate actions, to perform the function of governance in a variety of settings. These arrangements may be extremely simple, as in the case of informal social norms that grow up to govern the allocation of chores among the members of a household; they may also be highly complex, as in the cases of laws governing the production and dissemination of knowledge and the transfer of wealth through inheritance. But in every case the core elements of governance systems are social institutions in the sense of assemblages of rights, rules, and decision-making procedures that give rise to social practices, assign roles to the participants in these practices, and guide interactions among holders of these roles.[7] There is a pronounced tendency to equate the terms governance system and institution in common usage, but governance is a broader concept. Governance systems ordinarily encompass cognitive, cultural, and technological elements over and above their institutional cores. Arrangements governing the harvest of renewable resources, for instance, often reflect the discourse of conservation resting on the scientific foundation associated with the concept of sustainable yields. Social conventions are rooted for the most part in broader cultures, a condition that plays a prominent role when it comes to matters of compliance. Arrangements featuring area restrictions applicable to the activities of users depend on the availability of the technologies needed to monitor the activities of harvesters and verify that they are in compliance with the applicable rules.

Governance: Constitutive vs. Operational

In thinking about governance systems it is helpful to begin by drawing a distinction between constitutive arrangements and operational arrangements. Constitutive arrangements are broad frameworks comprised of systems of rights, rules, and decision-making procedures applicable across a range of more focused governance issues and capable of providing a foundation on which to construct more focused rules and procedures addressing specific issues, such as harvesting fish or trees, extracting oil and gas, and preventing pollution. Constitutive arrangements can and often do supply a variety of governance services on a centralized basis, including funding systems, compliance mechanisms, and dispute-resolution procedures, thereby relieving operational arrangements of the need to address such matters in issue-specific terms. At the national level these constitutive arrangements are normally articulated in the provisions of a constitution. The US Constitution, for example, has been interpreted in a way that allows it to provide common procedures for creating and administering regimes dealing with a broad spectrum of issues relating to the environment and natural resources as well as many other prominent concerns. In other cases constitutive arrangements are more rudimentary either because the social system has no constitution, as in many traditional small-scale societies, or because the relevant social system is less well developed with regard to governance, as in the case of international society.[8]

Even so, to assume that constitutive arrangements are entirely lacking in such cases would be a mistake. Research on traditional small-scale systems has revealed the existence of relatively sophisticated constitutive arrangements well known to their subjects even when they are informal in nature. The commonfield agriculture system—an arrangement under which village residents shared the use of surrounding fields—that flourished in medieval England, for example, operated within an overarching framework centered on the great landed estates, which provided services in such forms as manor courts to handle the resolution of disputes.[9] International society not only operates within the rules codified in the Charter of the United Nations; it also has constitutive arrangements covering several broad issue areas. The UN Convention on the Law of the Sea (UNCLOS), for instance, sets forth a broad framework governing human uses of marine resources and provides a foundation on which to build a variety of operational arrangements pertaining to fisheries, maritime commerce, environmental protection, the resolution of jurisdictional disputes, and so forth.[10] Somewhat similar remarks are in order regarding the framework embedded in the Antarctic Treaty, which has served as a platform for the development of operational arrangements dealing with a range of issues, including scientific research, fisheries, mining, tourism, and pollution, since it entered into force in 1961.[11]

Operational arrangements, by contrast, are more focused structures that build on constitutive arrangements to provide detailed systems of rights, rules, and decision-making procedures addressing specific issue areas or, in some cases, spatially demarcated regions. Familiar examples include regimes governing fishing and hunting, mining, oil and gas extraction, endangered species, and various forms of pollution at the national level. Counterparts in small-scale societies deal with matters like subsistence harvesting and the use of common pastures. At the international level there is a growing collection of operational arrangements covering matters like transboundary air pollution, stratospheric ozone depletion, climate change, transboundary rivers and lakes, marine pollution, migratory species, and biosafety, to name a few. For the most part operational arrangements differ from constitutive systems in terms of not only the detailed nature of their provisions but also adjustability. They are designed to be easier to adjust to changing circumstances than the constitutive arrangements on which they rest. Constitutive arrangements do change from time to time. Consider the establishment of Exclusive Economic Zones, a change in the public order of the oceans codified in the provisions of UNCLOS in 1982, under which coastal states gained jurisdiction over adjacent waters out to two hundred nautical miles. But the normal situation is one that allows for adjustments in operational arrangements to respond to changing needs for governance that do not call into question the constitutive foundations on which they rest. All sorts of changes in the regimes governing fisheries and air pollution in the United States, for instance, are made on a routine basis without calling into question any of the constitutive arrangements articulated in the Constitution.

The Formation of Governance Systems

Three distinct processes control the creation of governance systems: self-generation, bargaining, and imposition. Some systems of rights, rules, and decision-making procedures take the form of informal social practices arising as emergent properties of the behavior of groups of actors interacting in the absence of intentional initiatives on the part of anyone. They feature social norms or conventions around which expectations converge even though they are informal and not accompanied by explicit compliance mechanisms. Such self-generated arrangements are common in traditional societies and sometimes arise as alternatives to arrangements articulated in more formal, legal instruments even in modern societies. In larger and more formalized settings efforts to create governance systems regularly feature institutional bargaining, processes of negotiation in what are often thought of as mixed-motive or competitive-cooperative interactions.[12] All the participants in such interactions stand to gain from reaching an agreement on the terms of governance systems, but they have divergent preferences regarding the specific provisions of the bargains to be struck. Imposition, by contrast, takes over when some participants are in a position to use the control of political institutions or outright coercion to impose their preferences on others who have little choice but to accede to the dictates of the powerful.

These are analytic distinctions. The creation of governance systems under real-world conditions invariably involves a mix of these processes. Negotiations sometimes focus on efforts to formalize arrangements (e.g., the extension of the jurisdiction of states over coastal waters) that have emerged as informal practices or matters of customary law. Some participants in negotiations relating to the creation of governance systems have more bargaining power than others do and are therefore able to assert their preferences successfully in crafting the terms of agreements. Even those who are well endowed with the sources of power in the material sense may find it hard to resist shifts in the terms of prevailing discourses (e.g., the rise of the discourse of conservation with its associated doctrine of sustainable use during the twentieth century).[13] Nevertheless, it is helpful to bear in mind the differences among self-generation, negotiation, and imposition in seeking to understand the creation stories associated with specific governance systems.[14]

Dynamic Governance

Once established, governance systems do not become unchanging or static arrangements. All governance systems—but especially operational arrangements—are subject to change over time arising from shifts in the character of the problems to be solved, changes in the nature and capabilities of the actors involved, or developments in the broader setting, including the rise of new discourses and the emergence of new technologies. A number of distinct patterns of change in governance systems occur with some regularity.[15] These include progressive development, punctuated equilibrium, arrested development, diversion, and collapse. Specific systems may exhibit more than one pattern over the course of time. A governance system that moves from strength to strength during its early days can run into trouble and even collapse at a later stage. An arrangement that seems to be going nowhere initially can reach a tipping point that triggers a period of progressive development. The conditions that determine patterns of change arising in specific cases include a combination of attributes of the governance system itself and features of the broader biophysical and socioeconomic settings in which it operates. For the most part these developments take the form of emergent properties of complex systems that are difficult to foresee in advance, much less to control in an intentional manner.

Environmental Governance

Environmental governance is a proper subset of the larger domain of governance. This subset includes those cases of steering the actions of humans, both individually and collectively, that involve uses of natural resources or impacts on ecosystems. As a first approximation it is helpful to distinguish two broad classes of situations in which environmental governance becomes important: those involving the intentional use or appropriation of natural resources or ecosystem services and those in which human actions produce unintended side effects that impact the Earth's biophysical systems. The first of these categories includes all the familiar human uses of natural resources, such as fish, trees, minerals, and hydrocarbons. The second encompasses all the usual forms of pollution and ecosystem degradation generated as by-products of human actions undertaken for other purposes. In some cases the two categories are linked because human efforts to extract natural resources produce side effects involving pollution or the degradation of ecosystems in such forms as the destruction of benthic communities arising from bottom trawling, the elimination of critical habitat resulting from deforestation, or the degradation of land occurring as a by-product of hardrock mining. In all these cases the objective of governance is to guide human actions in such a way as to promote sustainability and avoid or reduce destructive side effects to the maximum extent possible.

Environmental or Resource Regimes

Governance systems that are specialized to the treatment of these concerns are known generally as environmental or resource regimes.[16] These arrangements, comprised of assemblages of rights, rules, decision-making procedures, and programmatic activities addressing human actions occurring in specific times and places, occur at all levels of social organization, from informal social practices that govern hunting and gathering in small-scale settings to regimes dealing with fishing and air pollution at the national level and on to arrangements focusing on trade in endangered species and climate change at the international level. Some environmental regimes are constitutive in nature; they provide broad frameworks covering a range of human activities, as in the cases of the organic act covering the management of national parks in the United States and the framework convention covering the management of human uses of marine systems at the international level. But the typical environmental or resource regime is issue specific, addressing matters like land use at the local level, air pollution at the national level, or the depletion of stratospheric ozone at the international level. Most of what I have to say about environmental governance in this book focuses on the nature and performance of these issue-specific regimes.

Environmental Problem Sets

Although every situation that gives rise to a need for governance is unique, it is helpful to start by identifying a number of classes or types of situations in which environmental regimes come into play. I call these problem sets. The most prominent of these deal with (i) collective-action problems, (ii) problems involving side effects, (iii) allocation problems, and (iv) problems of institutional interplay.

Collective-action problems arise whenever the actions of the members of a group that seem rational in individualistic terms generate outcomes that are undesirable for all members of the group.[17] With regard to environmental concerns, the classic examples are known as the tragedy of the commons and the free-rider problem.[18] The tragedy of the commons occurs when individual members of a group lack incentives to conserve a natural resource (e.g., a stock of fish or a common pasture), with the result that their actions lead to the depletion, degradation, or destruction of the resource in a manner harmful to all. The free-rider problem arises when individual members of a group stand to benefit from the supply of a public good (e.g., healthy ecosystems) but fail to contribute because they hope that others will cover the cost of providing the good, thereby supplying them with the good at no cost to themselves. In all such cases the essential role of governance is to introduce rights and rules that give individual group members incentives to use natural resources sustainably or to contribute to the supply of public goods.

Whether we label them *side effects, by-products, or externalities,* human actions regularly produce unintended and often unforeseen consequences that affect the well-being of others. With respect to human-environment relations, these consequences cover a range of matters like the loss of ecosystem services arising from the harvesting of trees for timber, the harmful effects of runoffs associated with agricultural production, the health effects of air and water pollution, and the impacts of emissions of greenhouse gases on the Earth's climate system.[19] As economists often remind us, externalities can be positive as well as negative. The harvest of timber, for instance, can produce habitat that is favorable for some species even as it leads to a loss of various ecosystem services. But in every case the challenge for governance in this realm is to devise mechanisms that lead actors to internalize these externalities, or, in other words, to take into account the costs and benefits of side effects or by-products in their decisions regarding the use of natural resources. Ideally, this would lead to a situation in which farmers would pay for the downstream impacts of fertilizers and pesticides, operators of power plants would pay for the effects of emissions of greenhouse gases, and shippers would pay for the environmental consequences of black carbon that diesel engines produce. Ultimately, end users would bear these costs in the form of higher prices for various products (e.g., food, electricity), an outcome that seems perfectly appropriate in most cases. Even where such full-cost accounting is not feasible, governance systems can and often do move collective behavior toward this ideal.

The *problem of allocation* is a matter of who gets what rather than a matter of sustainability or the avoidance of negative side effects. If catch shares are established in a fishery, how should we allocate these shares among users? If we place a cap on emissions of greenhouse gases, how should we allocate emissions permits? If we restrict the number of people allowed to enter a national park at a given time, how should we allocate entrance permits among members of the public desiring to visit the park? In some cases (e.g., catch shares) we deal with such matters through some form of grandfathering, a distribution of shares based on patterns of past use. But justifying practices of this sort on the basis of any reasonable principle of equity or fairness is often difficult. Equally important, once we put in place a system that generates revenue as a product of allocation (e.g., fees produced from auctioning permits to emitters of greenhouse gases), the question of how to allocate these revenues among various possible uses comes into focus. In making decisions about such matters governance systems must address questions of equity, implicitly if not explicitly.[20]

Institutional interplay refers to interactions between or among regimes operating at the same time. Horizontal interplay takes place at the same level of social interaction and encompasses both cases occurring within the same broad issue domain (e.g., the interplay between the ozone regime and the climate regime at the international level) and cases extending across two or more issue domains (e.g., interactions between the climate regime and the international trade regime). Vertical interplay, which features interactions crossing levels of social organization, gives rise to what is known as multilevel governance.[21] What is the division of authority and responsibility between state governments and the national government in addressing problems of air pollution? Can those responsible for administering international regimes count on member governments to implement the provisions of these arrangements (e.g., the regimes dealing with climate change and biodiversity) within their own jurisdictions? The challenge of governance in this realm is to devise procedures that allow individual regimes to operate effectively while minimizing mutual interference and finding ways to alleviate clashes when they do occur. The significance of this problem set has risen rapidly as a function of globalization; problems of this sort are destined to become matters of profound importance as we move deeper into a world of human-dominated ecosystems.

Performance of Environmental Regimes

Casual observation is sufficient to demonstrate that some environmental regimes are more successful than others. The US regime that was created to curb long-range air pollution arising from the operation of coal-fired power plants and the international regime that was established to phase out the production of ozone-depleting substances have met with considerable success. Conversely, the regimes created to reduce emissions of greenhouse gases and slow the rate of loss of biological diversity have not performed well. Going beyond such simple observations, however, we must ask, how should we assess the performance of environmental and resource regimes?

Regime Effectiveness

In every case the effectiveness of regimes—the extent to which the creation and operation of these governance systems produces results that differ from what would have happened in their absence—is a major focus of interest.[22] It is common to approach this concern at three distinct levels often described as outputs, outcomes, and impacts. Outputs refer to measures (e.g., the promulgation of regulations) taken to implement these arrangements in order to achieve a transition from paper to practice. Outcomes, by contrast, encompass changes in the behavior of those subject to a regime's provisions that can be attributed in a convincing manner to the operation of the regime. Finally, the concept of impacts refers to problem solving or the extent to which a regime plays a role in solving the (stated or unstated) problem that led to its creation.

Demonstrating the effectiveness of regimes in these terms is not easy, however. Outputs are the easiest of the three levels of effectiveness to document, but they are also the least important of the three. What we really want to know is the extent to which regimes play a causal role in solving problems arising in human-environment relations. But reaching clear-cut conclusions about impacts is difficult not only because of the existence of small numbers of cases and the lack of opportunities to conduct controlled experiments but also because regimes always interact with other forces that play a role in determining the course of human-environment relations. More often than not these forces interact in complex ways that make it difficult to assign precise weights to the causal significance of individual forces. Devising procedures that allow us to isolate the causal signal of environmental regimes or, for that matter, all social institutions is an ongoing challenge in efforts to understand the effectiveness of these arrangements. We have made progress in addressing this challenge, but there is much more to be done.[23]

Performance Standards

Assuming that regimes do make a difference, enquiring about their performance with respect to various normative standards becomes relevant.[24] Among the most prominent of these standards are efficiency, equity, and various conceptions of good governance. The idea of efficiency is simple, at least in conceptual terms. Is the regime cost effective in the sense that it minimizes the cost to society of solving the relevant problem? Equity is a more complex criterion. In distributive terms it directs attention to the extent to which the operation of a regime produces winners and losers and whether the pattern of these distributive consequences is fair or just. Is it fair, for example, to allocate permits to emit greenhouse gases to current emitters, or should these permits be auctioned off with the proceeds to go to the general public in some form? Other ways of thinking about equity spill over almost immediately into the sorts of concerns embedded in the notion of good governance. Among the most prominent of these concerns are participation, transparency, and accountability.[25] Are all relevant stakeholders given an opportunity to participate in the operation of a regime? Are its operations transparent to anyone willing to make an effort to scrutinize its performance? Are those responsible for administering the regime accountable to some public authority or to the affected public for the consequences of their actions? Applying these normative standards to the operations of specific regimes poses a range of complex challenges. But we can say at the outset that this sort of performance evaluation differs from the assessment of effectiveness. A regime may be highly successful—even solving the problem that led to its creation—yet fail to perform well in terms of one or more of these performance standards.

Generalizability

We know enough about environmental governance to realize that we need to go "beyond panaceas" when we create regimes to address specific problems.[26] Simple prescriptions—such as the propositions that creating property rights in natural resources will suffice to avoid the tragedy of the commons, that the presence of a dominant actor or what is known as a hegemon is necessary to create effective regimes, or that establishment of enforcement mechanisms able to deploy sanctions is necessary to make regimes effective—cannot withstand empirical testing. This has led to an emphasis on the idea of fit, or the extent to which a regime's features are well matched with the attributes of the problem it is created to solve.[27] Applied regime analysis must be rooted in what we have come to think of as "institutional diagnostics."[28] Just as an engineer asks many questions about the site and uses of a bridge before making recommendations about a suitable design, we need to know a good deal about the problem to be solved before making recommendations about the features of an appropriate regime.

Nevertheless, the issue of generalizability arises regularly in thinking about environmental governance. Are there generalizations about the creation and effectiveness of regimes that hold across a range of conditions? Or must we be content with the development of propositions about regimes whose applicability is severely limited?

These questions arise in three distinct forms: can we generalize about environmental governance across (i) levels of social organization, (ii) biophysically and culturally diverse settings, and (iii) issue domains?

Scaling Up/Down

To what extent can we scale up or down conclusions about environmental governance based on studies from the local level to the global level? This question has generated an ongoing dialogue between those whose work deals with small-scale regimes in culturally homogeneous settings and those who work on arrangements articulated in multilateral environmental agreements like the ozone regime.[29] These seemingly disparate settings have something in common because the phenomenon of governance without government is important in many small-scale traditional societies just as it is in international society. But there are also differences between these settings, not least regarding the role of cultural factors in determining the success of environmental regimes.

Natural and Cultural Diversity

Similar questions arise regarding the generalizability of propositions about environmental governance across biophysically and socioeconomically diverse settings. What can we learn from the success of the international regime dealing with stratospheric ozone depletion that may be relevant to improving the performance of the climate regime? Are there similarities between the climate regime and the regime dealing with biodiversity, despite the fact that one deals with what we think of as a systemic problem, whereas the other addresses a cumulative problem? Similar questions arise in thinking about environmental governance at other levels of social organization. Clearly, some conclusions do not generalize across settings that differ substantially in biophysical or socioeconomic terms. But it would be a mistake to give up on efforts to generalize across settings that differ in these terms just because some early efforts to pursue this goal have run into problems.

Issue Domains

Generalizing about governance across issue domains is another important challenge. Do findings about the effectiveness of environmental regimes apply to cases involving security, trade, or human rights?[30] Or to put it more concretely, do the insights we derive from analyzing international environmental regimes shed light on the performance of the international trade regime and vice versa? There are important differences among issue domains that should make us cautious about generalizing from one to another. The trade regime, for example, has access to the use of sanctions of a sort that are not available to most environmental regimes. Yet challenges like avoiding the tragedy of the commons and solving the free-rider problem arise in a wide range of issue domains; it does not make sense to give up on the search for generalizable propositions just because some significant differences among issue domains are apparent.

Plan of the Book

What follows is not a comprehensive account of environmental governance in all settings; rather, I seek to illuminate current understanding and key issues in this realm by working back and forth between the substantive concerns associated with governing human-environment relations and broader ideas about the nature of governance in general and the role of social institutions more specifically. For example, I draw on generic insights regarding the nature of collective-action problems to shed light on ways to avoid the tragedy of the commons in the harvesting of renewable resources while also looking to concrete examples relating to fish, forests, stratospheric ozone, and so forth to examine the pros and cons of different types of regimes available to address these problems in specific situations.

My story proceeds in three steps. Chapters 1 through 3 address what I call "simple environmental governance." These chapters look at human-environment relations regarding well-defined issues (e.g., harvesting fish, avoiding air pollution) that can be approached as more or less self-contained problems that do not spill over into other issue areas. Chapters 4 and 5 then turn to what I call "complex environmental governance," or situations in which problems are linked to one another in such a way that the establishment of regimes to address specific problems leads to institutional interplay (e.g., the interaction among regimes governing the use of land and water and regimes dealing with marine pollution). Chapters 6 and 7 direct attention to what I call "governance in the Anthropocene," a situation in which the emergence of human-dominated ecosystems has given rise to human-environment relations featuring systems dynamics that are often nonlinear, sometimes abrupt, and frequently irreversible.[31] The result is a set of challenges requiring the development of environmental regimes that are capable of governing effectively in turbulent times. The Conclusion turns to the question of making environmental governance work by joining analysis and praxis. How can we apply the products of our analytic efforts to contribute to solving problems on current policy agendas? Can the effort to solve these real-world problems contribute to the search for general propositions about environmental governance?

PART I

SIMPLE ENVIRONMENTAL GOVERNANCE

CHAPTER ONE
NATURAL RESOURCES

SOLVING COLLECTIVE-ACTION PROBLEMS

Collective-action problems are ubiquitous in human affairs. They arise whenever the members of a group make choices that seem rational from an individualistic perspective but turn out to produce outcomes that are undesirable for everyone.[1] The security dilemma in which nation-states engage in arms races fueled by efforts to counter one another's initiatives is a well-known example arising in the realm of world affairs, as is the failure of groups in domestic settings to band together to supply themselves with public goods, like secure neighborhoods or communal recreation facilities, even though all the members stand to benefit from the supply of such goods. Those seeking to elucidate the fundamental character of collective-action problems have devised a number of analytic constructs to aid thinking about such matters.[2] The most familiar approach centers on the game-theoretic model known as the prisoner's dilemma. A particularly striking feature of this construct is that each of the participants has a "dominant strategy," or, in other words, an option (generally referred to as "defect" in the literature on the prisoner's dilemma) that seems best regardless of the choices that others make. This means that avoiding or solving such problems is not simply a matter of providing the actors with information about the nature of the situation they face and making sure that they are aware of the existence of other, more cooperative options that can produce outcomes that are better for everyone; the concern about being exploited or becoming what is known as a "sucker" is too great in many cases to allow individuals to accept the risk that others may take advantage of their willingness to opt for a cooperative strategy.

Collective-action problems are just as prominent in the realm of human-environment relations as they are in other issue domains. The most striking cases involve what are known commonly as the tragedy of the commons and the free-rider problem. In the tragedy of the commons users of a resource (e.g., fish, forests, the capacity of biophysical systems to absorb wastes) deplete or overuse the resource because they are able to reap the benefits of doing so while incurring only a fraction of the costs of depleting or degrading the ecosystems in question. The essential challenge here is to find ways to limit the actions of individual users in the interests of achieving sustainability for all. In the case of the free-rider problem, by contrast, the difficulty involves persuading individual members of a group to contribute to the supply of public goods (e.g., the survival of charismatic species, a benign climate system). Even those who stand to reap net benefits if they make a contribution to the supply of such goods are likely to be tempted by the prospect that they can achieve even greater benefits if they are able to enjoy the public goods in question while leaving the cost of supplying them to others. The critical issue here is to create burden-sharing mechanisms that will generate sufficient contributions from the members of the group to cover the costs of supplying and, in some cases, maintaining the relevant public goods.

Formally, representing these problems in similar models is possible. They share the essential feature that what seems like a dominant strategy to those who assess their options in individualistic terms will lead to outcomes in which there are no winners. In thinking about environmental governance, however, there is much to be said for separating these problems and taking them up sequentially. The tragedy of the commons is the dominant concern of those who worry about the depletion or degradation of natural resources and devote their energy to devising ways to curb users' behavior that leads to these socially undesirable outcomes. Conversely, the free-rider problem looms large in the thinking of those who worry about the unwillingness of the members of a group to take the actions needed to supply themselves with a range of public goods like a stable climate or healthy and productive ecosystems. In this chapter I start with a discussion of strategies for avoiding the tragedy of the commons as it pertains to pursuing sustainability in the use of renewable resources. I then proceed to consider strategies for enhancing the willingness of group members to contribute to the supply of goods that everyone will enjoy once those goods become available to any member of the group.

The Tragedy of the Commons

Formalized in the 1950s in articles by Scott Gordon and Anthony Scott dealing with marine fisheries and popularized in Garrett Hardin's iconic 1968 *Science* article dealing with communal pastures, the idea of the tragedy of the commons has developed over the years into what is surely the best-known analytic construct dealing with human-environment relations.[3] The tragedy is treated as a product of the actions of human users of common pool resources. Such resources are both nonexcludable (once they become available to some members of a group, they are accessible to the others as well) and rival or subtractable (use on the part of individuals reduces the quantity or quality of the resources available for use on the part of other members of the group). The root of the problem lies in the fact that individual members of such groups lack incentives to conserve common pool resources either because others will snap up any units of the resource they leave or because they reap the full benefits but bear only a fraction of the costs associated with using the resource. Acting on the basis of individual incentives, therefore, group members will continue to use such resources until those resources are severely depleted/degraded and, in some cases, driven to extinction/exhaustion. Many observers have concluded that tragedies of this sort are common occurrences in a wide variety of social settings and that avoiding or ameliorating such problems is the central challenge of environmental governance.

Rights, Rules, and Common Pools

How persuasive is this line of reasoning? To answer this question, it is helpful to begin with several clarifying observations about the nature of common-pool resources and the circumstances of those humans who use them.[4] So long as the supply of a common-pool resource (e.g., a stock of fish, a pasture for cattle) is sufficient to meet the needs of all the human users/appropriators without degrading the quality of the resource or driving up the costs of harvesting, the tragedy will not occur. In situations in which the ratio of supply to demand is favorable, in fact, users are likely to band together to harvest the relevant resource in a cooperative manner that meets the needs of all and improves efficiency. There are many examples of sustainable systems of this sort in small-scale societies organized around various forms of hunting and gathering.[5] The question now is whether the growth of human populations and the rise of lifestyles featuring high levels of material consumption have created conditions on a global scale in which the supply-demand ratio has tilted so far in the other direction that no existing practices relating to the use of common-pool resources can yield sustainable results.

There are also questions about what is and is not a common pool resource. Stretching supplies of resources (e.g., freshwater) by using them more efficiently is often possible; advanced technologies may reduce the demand for a particular natural resource (e.g., bandwidth in the geomagnetic spectrum). Still, rivalness is a fairly straightforward condition; it occurs whenever one user's enjoyment of a resource reduces the quantity or quality of the resource available to others. But this is not the case when it comes to nonexcludability. With regard to renewable resources, like fish and game, there is a long history of efforts to introduce exclusion mechanisms, such as use rights and regulations intended to impose restrictions on the actions of potential users. The introduction of restrictions such as individual transferable quotas (ITQs) or catch shares can transform a fish stock that was once a common-pool resource into a resource featuring effective exclusion mechanisms. The creation of transferable emissions permits covering emissions of SO_2 or NO_x can change the atmosphere from a common-pool resource for disposing of the relevant wastes into a resource in which effective use rights govern the actions of human users. Both the feasibility and the cost of introducing exclusion mechanisms vary as a function of the attributes of the resource, the imaginativeness of managers, and the skills of political leaders. It may turn out, for example, that devising effective exclusion mechanisms to deal with the use of the atmosphere treated as a repository for emissions of greenhouse gases is particularly difficult or costly. Yet once the political will to tackle this issue arises, key players will likely find ways to create exclusion mechanisms that will transform this common-pool resource into a resource that prospective users will have to pay to use. For the most part common-pool resources are socially constructed. What was once a resource of this type can be turned into a resource of another type through the creation of exclusion mechanisms.

Solution Strategies

Empirical research has made it clear that something like the tragedy of the commons occurs under some conditions but not others.[6] What are these conditions, and what strategies are available to those who wish to avoid or ameliorate the tragedy in specific situations? Broadly speaking, three types or families of strategies have emerged in efforts to address this challenge.[7] Each is associated with a distinctive structure of property rights, and each directs attention to a different mechanism for avoiding the tragedy. For purposes of discussion we can characterize these strategies as (i) the rise of social conventions or norms guiding behavior in common property systems, (ii) the emergence of incentives for individual users to conserve resources in private property systems, and (iii) the development of regulatory arrangements governing behavior in public property systems. Some analysts seek to compare and contrast the performance of these strategies in the hope of coming up with *the solution* to the tragedy of the commons. But the principal conclusions emerging from a large and growing body of research in this field are that each of the mechanisms has advantages and disadvantages; more than one of the mechanisms may suffice to avoid the tragedy in specific situations, and the choice of a particular mechanism in any given case is apt to be as much a matter of political culture as of the objective merits of particular solutions.

Some of those concerned about the tragedy of the commons equate common property with social practices allowing for unrestricted or open-to-entry access to resources on the part of all those actors who are members of the ownership group. But this is an extreme case that is uncommon in developed governance systems featuring common property. In the more typical case social conventions or norms evolve—explicitly or implicitly—that impose duties on users and spell out well-defined procedures for limiting harvests and regulating the distribution of resources when supply is insufficient to satisfy the demands of all those desiring to use the resources.[8] The resultant social practices are normally rooted in established cultures that determine who is entitled to harvest the resources, how the harvest is to be distributed among members of the relevant social group, and what measures are available to ensure that individual members comply with the norms embedded in these practices. These practices yield sustainable results in a wide variety of real-world situations, but there is no guarantee that they will always produce socially desirable outcomes in human-environment interactions. Broadly speaking, it is fair to say that this way of avoiding the tragedy of the commons will run into trouble when nonlinear and abrupt changes in biophysical systems require rapid adaptation to shifting conditions and when the relevant cultures are underdeveloped (e.g., in the case of international society) or compromised due to the impact of outside forces beyond their control (e.g., the spread of colonialism). Nonetheless, the evidence is clear that common-property systems have produced sustainable results in a variety of settings featuring distinct patterns of resource use and different types of social practices. Key questions regarding strategies featuring some form of common property include the extent to which such practices can hold up under the pressures arising from population growth and globalization and the degree to which such solutions can work under conditions of modernization or at higher levels of social organization ranging up to the level of global systems, as in cases like protecting the Earth's climate system.

Privatization offers an alternative approach to avoiding or solving the tragedy of the commons that appeals to those who are accustomed to operating in settings in which private property systems are prominent or even predominant social institutions.[9] Strategies of this kind involve introducing exclusion mechanisms that make it possible to provide individual members of the group with secure property rights in the resource. This results in creating bundles of rights that may include proprietary, use, exclusion, and disposition rights and whose actual content varies considerably from one case to another. The core idea is that privatization will alter the incentives of individual users in desirable ways. Harvesters will have incentives to limit their take when they know that units of the resource (e.g., fish, trees) they leave today will be available to them in the future and that they will bear the full costs as well as reap the benefits arising from the use of the resource (e.g., parcels of grazing land). This approach to solving the tragedy of the commons has well-known attractions, but it also has real or potential drawbacks. Owners of natural resources may decide to liquidate them entirely, investing the proceeds in alternative activities that seem more profitable to them regardless of the views of the broader community.[10] When the rights in question (e.g., catch shares in the fisheries) do not include the authority to set allowable harvest levels, privatization may still lead to overuse or degradation of resources. Market failures may lead to outcomes that are inequitable or violate other community standards. The actions of owners may generate more or less severe side effects (e.g., the disruption of ecosystems critical to other living resources) that owners of a given resource are free to ignore in making decisions about the use of the resources they own. The results may violate pertinent standards of fairness or justice, either because the initial allocation of resources among members of the ownership group is inequitable or because such arrangements give owners an unfair advantage over other members of the social group. None of these problems is an inevitable consequence of privatization; in specific situations, those who are alert to the dangers, possess the authority needed to address these problems, and are prepared to take vigorous steps to exercise this authority can avoid or overcome many of the challenges. Nevertheless, empirical research on cases in which groups adopt some form of privatization as a strategy for avoiding the tragedy of the commons makes it clear that privatization is not a panacea under real-world conditions. Despite—or perhaps because of—the fact that privatization appeals to many on what are basically ideological grounds, therefore, it is critical to examine the pros and cons of this family of solutions to the tragedy on a case-by-case basis.

This brings us to strategies featuring public property as a means of avoiding or solving the tragedy of the commons. The core idea here is simple: if the state owns land and natural resources and if the agents employed by the state to manage human uses of these resources can be counted on to act in the public interest, it is possible to establish and implement rules and regulations that would limit uses of the resources in the interests of achieving sustainable outcomes and ensuring that the public reaps benefits in such forms as lease sales, royalties, and user fees imposed on individual or corporate users. As with the other strategies, there are many real-world situations in which arrangements of this sort produce socially desirable outcomes. But here too there are pitfalls.[11] Special interests may capture regulatory agencies or exert undue influence over their behavior. Regulatory systems are subject to problems of inability to determine optimal use rates, bureaucratic sluggishness, and institutional arthritis that become more severe with the passage of time. Public resources are sometimes simply given away on the basis of arguments that are ideological in character or made available to private users on a heavily subsidized basis. Nor is public ownership a guarantee that uses of natural resources will conform to community standards of equity or justice. A special case arises with regard to rivers, coastal and marine areas, and airspace managed by public authorities, despite the fact that they are not, strictly speaking, part of the public domain. Resources of this sort are commonly subject to some sort of public trust doctrine that authorizes and even obligates the state to make arrangements for their management.[12] As in the cases of common property and private property, the bottom line here is that public property systems produce socially desirable outcomes under some conditions but not under others.

The Problem of Allocation

It is worth noting that solving the tragedy of the commons in the sense of avoiding the degradation or exhaustion of natural resources does not ensure that the outcomes will conform to reasonable standards of fairness, equity, or good governance. How should catch shares be allocated among those wishing to use a renewable resource like fish? Where privatization is the strategy chosen for avoiding the tragedy, what elements should bundles of property rights include and how should these bundles be distributed among the members of the relevant society? Is it possible to structure regulations promulgated by governments so as to treat fairly the claims of distinct groups within society? The problem of allocation has received less attention than the problem of avoiding the degradation or exhaustion of resources, but it turns out to be a critical determinant of the success of efforts to avoid or solve the tragedy of the commons in a wide range of settings.[13] There is a pronounced tendency in many settings to grandfather the rights of current users at the time an environmental regime is established. However, both normative reasoning and real-world experience makes it clear that this approach, which may be expedient in political terms, leaves a great deal to be desired in many cases in terms of any reasonable standard of fairness or equity. The result quite often is a pattern of protracted battles during the course of implementing a new regime and festering dissatisfaction that can cause serious threats to the effectiveness of the regime over time.[14]

Two principal conclusions emerge from this account of the main approaches to avoiding or solving the tragedy of the commons. We need to be alert to the gap between the ideal and the actual in every case and avoid inappropriate comparisons between ideal forms of one or another of the strategies and actual forms of the others. Each family of strategies can produce results that are desirable in terms of criteria of sustainability but only if they are designed with the problem of fit in mind. Social norms that are not linked to effective compliance mechanisms cannot produce sustainable results. Systems of private property that do not include duties or obligations to respect the rights of neighboring owners or the general public will lead to outcomes featuring collateral damage and fail to conform to standards of fairness and good governance. Iron triangles in which representatives of user groups, public agencies, and legislative bodies collude to promote special interests over the public interest lead to undesirable outcomes regarding the use of natural resources just as they do in other issue areas. The other conclusion is that it is essential to bear in mind considerations of equity and good governance in such settings rather than to focus only on sustainability in biophysical terms. Regimes created to solve the tragedy of the commons that many members of the relevant society regard as unfair or inequitable will be vulnerable to festering opposition that can flare up in ways that undermine the effectiveness of these arrangements. A failure to take the requirements of good governance seriously will only fan the flames of lasting dissent.

The Free-Rider Problem

Consider now a second collective-action problem that challenges our ability to govern human-environment relations effectively, commonly known as the free-rider problem. The central concern here focuses on the supply of goods and services that share with common-pool resources the attribute of nonexcludability but that differ from them in the sense that they are nonrival. This means that all members of a social group can enjoy the benefits flowing from such goods without diminishing the enjoyment of others. Nature supplies some public goods. Amenities (e.g., picturesque landscapes, charismatic megafauna) in contrast to commodities often exhibit these characteristics.[15] For instance, the enjoyment I derive from knowing that polar bears exist does not detract from your enjoyment of their existence. So long as these goods remain nonrival, the tragedy of the commons is not a concern. The principal challenge in such cases is to avoid the degradation or destruction of these goods as an unintended consequence of actions taken to fulfill other objectives (a topic to which I return in the next chapter). The threat to polar bears arising from the impacts of climate change exemplifies this concern.

Of more immediate concern are situations in which there is a need for coordinated or concerted actions in order to supply public goods that nature does not provide. The restoration of ecosystems degraded by anthropogenic actions, for example, involves the supply of public goods in the form of ecosystem services that everyone can enjoy once some member(s) of the group take(s) the initiative required to supply them. Efforts to eliminate or ameliorate threats to the stratospheric ozone layer or the climate system also provide familiar examples. Once society takes effective action to protect the ozone layer, for instance, everyone will benefit from protection against ultraviolet radiation as a public good.

Whenever concrete actions are needed to supply a public good (including the introduction of prohibitions such as a ban on discarding trash in public places), the free-rider problem becomes a matter of serious concern. Individual members of the group who will benefit from the supply of the good, even if they are required to contribute toward the cost of supplying it, will stand to benefit even more if others make the contributions needed to cover the cost of supply while those individuals become free-riders who enjoy the same benefits without making a contribution. If each member of the group reasons in this way, the relevant public good will not be supplied, despite the fact that all members of the group would stand to benefit even if required to contribute to the cost of supplying it. As in the case of the tragedy of the commons, individual members commonly find that they have dominant strategies in such situations. If others contribute, the individual has an incentive to behave as a free-rider. If, however, others fail to contribute, the individual has an incentive to refrain from contributing to a losing cause. When everyone reasons in this way, no one will receive the public good, an outcome that is undesirable for all.[16]

Conceptual Clarifications

Before turning to a discussion of strategies for solving or ameliorating this problem as it arises in human-environment relations, a few clarifications are in order. There are cases in which it is possible to solve the free-rider problem by introducing exclusion mechanisms. An owner of public goods (e.g., a park located on public land) can take steps to introduce exclusion mechanisms (e.g., a system of user fees), generating both incentives and resources needed to protect these goods in the process. Goods that are nonrival up to a point (e.g., a natural area that is particularly attractive for bird watching) can become congested when too many people want to use it at the same time, thereby eroding the quality of nonrivalness that is a defining characteristic of public goods. Members of a social group may differ in their evaluation of goods that are nonexcludable and nonrival. In extreme cases some members of the group may regard such goods as public "bads" whereas others remain convinced that they are public goods. Management systems that do an excellent job of ensuring that harvests of elephants or whales are sustainable exemplify this possibility. Although conservationists are likely to hail such systems as important achievements in the realm of human-environment relations, preservationists opposed to any killing of megafauna will regard the same systems as public bads.[17] As is true in the case of common pool resources, then, the boundaries of the category of public goods are often socially constructed. What is a public good under some conditions may turn out to be excludable, rival, or both under other conditions.

Solution Strategies

Focusing on those cases in which the free-rider problem is a major concern (e.g., restoring degraded ecosystems on a local scale to mitigating climate change on a global scale), what strategies are available to overcome this problem of collective action? Here too at least three streams of thinking are worth differentiating: (i) the emergence of a dominant actor, or what is commonly known as a hegemon, (ii) the rise of mechanisms that encourage individual members of the group to contribute by providing them with selective incentives, and (iii) the negotiation of burden-sharing agreements combined with effective compliance mechanisms.

A dominant actor in this setting is a single member of the relevant group who values a public good more than the total cost of supplying it.[18] Such an individual would be able and, if necessary, willing to cover the cost of supplying the good even if all the other members of the group were to behave as free-riders. Situations of this sort may arise in a variety of settings, ranging from cases in which a good neighbor keeps the common yard in good order to cases in which a nation-state is prepared to undertake the effort needed to eliminate or ameliorate pollution in a transboundary water body. Research on environmental governance suggests that groups of this sort, commonly known as privileged groups, do occur at a number of levels of social organization, especially in what are known as "single-best effort" situations, in which an initial push can supply the good to members of the relevant group once and for all.[19] Nonetheless, it would be naive to expect this solution to the free-rider problem to prove effective in more than a small fraction of the situations in which this problem arises. In the typical case no individual member of the group will have the resources or the capacity to supply the relevant public goods on its own or to supply the socially optimal amount of the public goods, especially in cases in which these goods are lumpy in the sense that they must be supplied in discrete units or not at all. Equally important is the observation that a hegemon can be expected to follow its own preferences in deciding on the character of the public good to be supplied. This may produce mutually acceptable outcomes in cases in which the hegemon is benign or public spirited in the sense that it seeks to supply public goods that conform to the preferences of the members of the group to the maximum degree possible. But hegemons may well seem malign rather than benign from the perspective of other members of the group. Although this may be an issue of limited concern when the stakes are low (e.g., in deciding what types of flowers to plant in the communal garden), it is easy to see that the actions of a malign hegemon can become a matter of intense concern to other members of the group when preferences diverge sharply (e.g., in cases in which group members disagree on the merits of conservation vs. preservation in managing charismatic species).[20] In such cases other members of the group may treat the goods in question as public bads and devote time and energy to thwarting the efforts of the hegemon.

Another strategy for alleviating the free-rider problem focuses on what are known as selective incentives, excludable benefits that can be provided to individual members of a group as a reward for contributing to the supply of public goods. Developed in the effort to explain the creation of labor unions, this line of thinking directs attention to things like insurance policies or certain types of health care that unions (or other organized groups) can provide to their members along with pubic goods such as minimum wage laws or regulations regarding working conditions.[21] Are selective incentives relevant to the realm of environmental governance? Particularly striking examples of this phenomenon arise in connection with funding environmental nongovernmental organizations, or ENGOS (e.g., the Environmental Defense Fund, Greenpeace, the Worldwide Fund for Nature). The raison d'être of these organizations is to provide the public with public goods in such forms as the protection of endangered species or the preservation of wilderness areas. But they regularly offer donors private goods, such as items like T-shirts, tote bags, coffee mugs, and so forth, as rewards for their contributions. There is no doubt that selective incentives are a significant part of the story when it comes to solving the free-rider problem with respect to environmental goods, yet this discussion suggests both that selective incentives may energize the efforts of some actors rather than the group as a whole and that the scope for the operation of this mechanism will be limited in relation to the magnitude of the environmental problems (e.g., climate change, loss of biodiversity) that now loom large on the environmental agenda.

This brings us to the negotiation of burden-sharing arrangements as a strategy for solving the free-rider problem in the effort to supply environmental public goods. The fundamental idea here is straightforward: faced with the need to overcome the free-rider problem, the members of a social group or, more often, a subset of the most influential members or a small number of negotiating blocs can engage in a bargaining process designed to agree on both the defining characteristics of the public good to be supplied and the nature of a funding mechanism created to cover the cost of supplying the good.[22] Whereas participants in efforts to supply private goods generally seek to form minimum-winning coalitions, bargaining over the supply of public goods typically features efforts to form maximum-winning coalitions. Because private goods are excludable and rival, those seeking to make arrangements for their supply will want to minimize the number of actors who have legitimate claims to a share of the proceeds. In the case of goods that are nonexcludable and non-rival, by contrast, there is every reason to draw as many contributors as possible into coalitions that form in order to ensure that the goods are supplied at a socially desirable level.[23] Among other things, this makes it important to address considerations of equity or fairness in building support for the supply of public goods. The resultant negotiations do produce mutually acceptable outcomes under some conditions, but the transaction costs associated with this type of institutional bargaining are often high, a fact that may lead to the formation of a leadership coalition (often called a "k group") to avoid excessive delays in the supply of public goods combined with the hope that, as time passes, additional participants can be drawn into the coalition of contributors.[24]

Assuming the relevant actors succeed in reaching agreement on the features of the public good to be supplied and on an acceptable burden-sharing arrangement, what incentives do the members of such a coalition have to comply with their commitments when it comes to implementing the agreement? In domestic settings such agreements may take the form of contractual or other legally binding obligations so that it is possible to threaten those who fail to live up to their obligations with various types of sanctions. But empirical studies suggest both that sanctions are not the only factor affecting compliance in domestic settings and that other factors may prove effective in eliciting compliant behavior even in settings (e.g., international society) in which sanctions in the ordinary sense are not available to induce parties to live up to their obligations.[25] Among these factors are a concern for one's reputation as a reliable partner in other settings, normative or ethical considerations associated with the logic of appropriateness, and the habit of obedience arising from some form of socialization.[26] None of these factors may prove sufficient to ensure compliance in specific situations. Still, it would be a mistake to assume that parties will always fail to live up to commitments to contribute to the supply of environmental public goods (e.g., restoring polluted water bodies, protecting the stratospheric ozone layer) in the absence of conventional enforcement mechanisms.

Like the tragedy of the commons, the free-rider problem involves a dilemma of collective action in which the members of a group who think about their choices in purely individualistic terms have dominant strategies that produce outcomes that are undesirable for all members of the group. Yet empirical evidence presents a mixed picture in which some groups succeed in supplying themselves with (adequate levels of) public goods, whereas others fail to supply themselves with such goods or end up with highly suboptimal levels of supply. With respect to environmental public goods like healthy and productive ecosystems or a climate system conducive to human well-being, then, the interesting questions have to do with the determinants of success or failure in this realm. There are undoubtedly situations in which a dominant actor takes steps to supply public goods or selective incentives are strong enough to persuade individuals to make contributions toward the supply of such goods. But these mechanisms are unlikely to produce satisfactory results in a range of situations involving the protection of endangered species, the restoration of degraded ecosystems, or the control of greenhouse gas emissions. Such cases will require negotiating burden-sharing agreements that are accompanied by mechanisms that are effective in inducing key actors to live up to their obligations. Because conventional enforcement mechanisms are frequently either inadequate or unavailable in such settings, efforts to understand and bring to bear alternative ways to elicit compliance will loom large in thinking about ways to supply environmental public goods during the foreseeable future.

Conclusion

Regimes created to avoid the tragedy of the commons or to solve the free-rider problem are themselves public goods.[27] Individual members of the group may differ greatly in their preferences regarding the content of such regimes. The intense debates over the introduction of limited-entry systems in marine fisheries and fees imposed on users of public lands constitute good examples of the controversies that arise in this realm. But the fact remains that regimes are intended to be nonexcludable and nonrival within the confines of the social groups in which they operate. This means that it is always important to avoid free-rider behavior when establishing environmental regimes and especially when moving these regimes from paper to practice over time. In the absence of a benign hegemon willing to take on this function largely out of self-interest, this will place a premium on building maximum-winning coalitions, a fact that directs attention to the importance of considerations of equity and good governance as determinants of the effectiveness of environmental governance systems.

Under the circumstances the fact that not only by the logic of consequences but also the logic of appropriateness influences the members of many groups is good news. One way to look at the role of social norms and various forms of socialization in human affairs is to see them as mechanisms for avoiding or solving dilemmas of collective action. Typically, these mechanisms evolve over time and are difficult to adjust quickly. In stable situations in which collective-action problems remain more or less unchanged over long periods of time, this does not pose a significant problem. But in a world where both biophysical and socioeconomic systems are subject to nonlinear, abrupt, and irreversible changes, there may not be time to wait for slow processes like the evolution of social norms and the effects of socialization. In later chapters I return to this topic and argue that this is one of the central problems we now face in the realm of environmental governance. New needs for governance arise at a pace that greatly exceeds that of familiar processes for adapting or replacing existing governance systems to meet them.

CHAPTER TWO
ENVIRONMENTAL PROTECTION

COPING WITH UNINTENDED SIDE EFFECTS

Whereas collective-action problems arise when decisions based on individualistic calculations produce outcomes that are undesirable for everyone, side effects occur when actions on the part of an individual member of a group motivated by a desire to enhance his or her own well-being produce unintended consequences or side effects that impinge on the welfare of others. Treating these side effects as externalities, economists regularly point out that their impacts may be positive as well as negative from the perspective of those whose well-being is affected. Others may benefit free of charge from the efforts of inventers to come up with new technologies, for example, so long as exclusion mechanisms are not in place. The rationale for introducing systems of patents centers on a desire to enhance the incentives of inventers to engage in socially desirable activities by allowing them to reap rewards from the benefits that their activities accrue for others. If successful, these arrangements internalize positive externalities, thereby ensuring that innovators are motivated to keep on with their work. In thinking about environmental protection, however, the more common concern centers on negative side effects or unintended harms that the self-interested actions of individuals inflict on other members of the group or on the group as a whole. Limited largely to local consequences in earlier times, such environmental impacts now arise in many settings and can affect the well-being of others up to the global level through occurrences like climate change and the loss of biological diversity.

Environmental side effects of interest today come in many forms. A prominent category includes problems of pollution ranging from the effects of hazardous waste sites on the health of local residents to the contamination of groundwater located in large aquifers, airborne pollutants that are precursors to acid rain, and on up to emissions of the greenhouse gases that cause climate change. But this is not the only category of side effects of interest to those who think about environmental governance. Another major category includes the disruption or destruction of habitat for other species resulting from the degradation of grazing lands associated with ranching and the degradation of benthic communities associated with industrial fishing. Here the actions of some users of natural resources have the effect of damaging co-located resources of interest to others. Yet another category of harmful side effects arises when the actions of those interested in harvesting or extracting commodities take a toll on the well-being of those who enjoy amenities, or values derived from nonconsumptive uses of natural resources. Clear-cutting forests or removing mountain tops to mine coal, for example, can cause irrevocable harm to ecosystems valued by many who are not interested in commodities like timber and coal. New types of side effects that inflict harm on the well-being of others arise with considerable regularity. A current example centers on the creation of wind farms, a development justified by the need to reduce reliance on fossil fuels as a measure to limit climate change but opposed by many because wind machines destroy scenic views, generate noise pollution, and lead to unintended stress on local infrastructure.

The challenge to governance in coping with all these side effects is to devise mechanisms to internalize environmental externalities in ways that enhance social welfare while at the same time are sensitive to the requirements of equity and good governance. We have come a long way from early efforts to address these needs through the development of the nuisance doctrine as a means for sorting out tensions arising between neighbors whose self-interested actions inflict harm on one another. We must find ways now to cope with massive, long-distance effects like emissions of sulfur dioxide that produce acid rain hundreds of miles from their sources and flows of agricultural fertilizers and pesticides that wash down rivers to produce dead zones in distant marine ecosystems. In analytic terms we can identify several families of strategies for coping with environmental side effects: one that involves granting rights to potential victims, a second that emphasizes the role of public authorities in developing rules governing the actions of those whose activities may inflict harm on others, and a third that seeks alternatives to the focus on rights and rules. The next three sections of this chapter examine these strategies in some detail. Subsequent sections then turn to issues of environmental justice and good governance arising from the use of these strategies under real-world conditions.

Victim's Rights

One way to address the problem of environmental side effects is to grant potential victims rights that they can exercise to deter harmful actions or to claim compensation once harmful actions take place. Articulated in many cases in the form of common law rooted in judicial opinions, the purpose of such rights is to level the playing field between the (typically property) rights of those whose actions prove harmful to others and the rights of those whose well-being is impaired as a result of those actions. The origins of this approach to coping with side effects lie in what is known as nuisance law, a body of principles fashioned initially to deal with injuries sustained as a result of negligence on the part of property owners but then developed over time to apply to a growing array of actions on the part of public as well as private actors.[1] The use of this strategy requires a well-defined perpetrator, an easily identifiable victim, and a convincing causal narrative linking the actions of the perpetrator to the harm the victim has experienced. In situations in which these conditions are met it is possible to develop liability rules governing the relationship between perpetrators and victims. Not surprisingly, the law dealing with liability rules has become highly complex and subject to a variety of interpretations in many real-world situations. But the underlying rationale is clear: those who suffer from the harmful effects of the self-interested actions of others should have some legal recourse to protect themselves in such situations.

In reality this strategy for coping with environmental side effects involves complex and often difficult trade-offs. Owners seeking to maximize gains from the use of their property will perceive liability rules designed to protect potential victims as more or less severe restrictions on their own rights. In extreme cases they will assert that these restrictions amount to regulatory or judicial takings of their property and thus seek compensation from society for losses in the value of their assets.[2] Balancing the two sets of claims is never easy. It can require complex and sometimes convoluted reasoning to arrive at clear-cut decisions in specific cases, and appeals of decisions handed down by lower courts can make the process of resolving such problems lengthy and costly. Furthermore, society may have significant interests in such situations that transcend the interests of those who are direct parties to interactions of this sort. Where the problem arises from the side effects of mining bauxite or iron ore, for instance, policy-makers may conclude that societal interests in economic growth or national security are sufficiently important to justify such activities, regardless of their side effects. In such cases the issue then becomes a matter of whether society as a whole—in contrast to the initial perpetrator—must assume an obligation to compensate those whose welfare is affected by the relevant activities.

Real-World Complications

All these matters become much more complex when (i) the victims are numerous and unorganized or poorly organized, (ii) the victims are located at some distance from the source of the harm, (iii) the harm to the victims is not of a material nature, and (iv) there is a lack of consensus regarding the causal mechanism involved. Consider cases involving acid rain or the extermination of species in this connection. Although these are certainly environmental side effects, there are apt to be thousands or even millions of victims whose health is affected in ways that are difficult to document conclusively or whose well-being is diminished in a manner that is not material in nature. In such cases questions relating to legal standing (i.e., who is entitled to initiate legal action), jurisdiction (i.e., which courts have authority regarding the matter), and the identity of the perpetrators (i.e., who is responsible for the harm inflicted) become critical and often contentious matters. There may also be complications regarding the availability of remedies in the event that courts find in favor of the victims in specific cases. For the most part courts rely on remedies involving the award of compensation to victims and the imposition of fines on perpetrators. But if my welfare is diminished as a consequence of the prospect that climate change will cause polar bears to go extinct, conventional remedies are likely to prove inadequate. None of this leads to the conclusion that strategies for coping with environmental side effects that feature victim's rights are ineffective or even irrelevant in a wide range of situations. But it does make it clear that this approach can constitute only one element in a larger tool kit when it comes to efforts to cope with environmental side effects under contemporary conditions.

Regulatory Measures

If the articulation of victim's rights is limited as a strategy for coping with environmental side effects, what is the alternative? Society can take steps to impose rules, including both prohibitions and requirements, on those whose actions are or may prove harmful to others.[3] Unlike victim's rights, which require the identification of specific victims and are apt to be applied through judicial mechanisms, rules are commonly formulated as general prescriptions that apply to designated categories of actors and activities and that require administrative capacity to move them from paper to practice. Such strategies are attractive not only because they can impose restrictions on the actors' behavior before any harm is done but also because they can be used as mechanisms for pursuing broad societal goals that are not easy to associate with the rights of individuals.

There are cases in which rules of this sort arise spontaneously or in the absence of action on the part of any entity (e.g., a legislative body) authorized to address such matters on behalf of society.[4] Social norms, backed by taboos or various forms of social pressure, take this form in many traditional societies. But as Robert Ellickson's work on "governance without law" makes clear, self-generated rules pertaining to environmental side effects also arise in contemporary settings. His case study centers on the development of informal rules governing interactions between suburban residents and cattle ranchers in Shasta County, California.[5] But there is no reason to treat this as a unique or even an exceptional situation; there are other cases in which the members of social groups find ways to formulate rules governing situations of this sort on their own and work out procedures for applying these rules to specific situations.

Nevertheless, the more common approach to developing such rules focuses on the provisions of laws adopted by an authoritative legislative body in domestic settings (e.g., the US Congress) or negotiated in the form of intergovernmental agreements at the international level. All arrangements of this sort involve a series of three interconnected steps. A legislative process leads to the formulation of the relevant rules in the form of a law (e.g., the Clean Air Act Amendments of 1990 in the United States) or a formal agreement (e.g., the 1987 Montreal Protocol on Substances that Deplete the Ozone Layer). An administrative process led by a designated agency (e.g., the Environmental Protection Agency in the United States) turns these rules into more detailed regulations and promulgates them as operational guidelines for those whose actions are covered by the rules. And a legal procedure (e.g., the court system in the United States) is established to resolve disagreements when disputes arise regarding the extent to which specific actors are behaving in a manner inconsistent with the regulations in concrete situations. The effectiveness of these mechanisms varies from one social setting and from one situation to another. The authority of the EPA to regulate emissions of carbon dioxide under the terms of the Clean Air Act, for instance, is a matter of ongoing disagreement. The availability of judicial mechanisms to resolve international disputes regarding the meaning of provisions of conventions or treaties is limited. Still, governance systems created to cope with environmental side effects must devise formal procedures or informal practices to handle all three of these functions if they are to succeed in addressing such problems.

Command-and-Control Regulations

The traditional approach to rule making in this realm features what are generally known as command-and-control regulations.[6] These are more or less precise prohibitions and requirements that call for specific actions on the part of those whose behavior is deemed likely to generate environmental side effects. They may, for example, require operators of coal-fired power plants to install scrubbers on their smokestacks, mandate shipbuilders to include segregated ballast tanks in oil tankers, or impose height restrictions on the construction of commercial buildings. Rule making of this sort quickly gives rise to a vast array of prescriptions requiring actors to behave in certain ways and prohibiting them from behaving in others. The result is the development of a growing bureaucracy needed to administer environmental regulations together with increasing difficulties in ensuring that the relevant actors comply with the terms of the regulations.

A powerful critique of command-and-control regulations, articulated with particular force by environmental economists, asserts that this approach to rule making is bound to produce inefficient results.[7] Those subject to such regulations must adopt the prescribed approach even when they may be able to achieve results that are as good or better using some less expensive method of dealing with the problem. Once they act to comply with a regulatory command, subjects will have no incentive to engage in additional steps to control or eliminate the relevant problem. Subjects who must comply with command-and-control regulations will not have incentives to form alliances or partnerships to reduce the net costs of reducing pollution or avoiding other environmental side effects. Over time, this line of thinking, which began as a critique of the orthodox approach to coping with side effects, came to dominate much thinking about how to tackle the problem of harmful side effects. By the 1990s it provided the rationale for a variety of policy initiatives covering an array of issues ranging from the introduction of permits covering emissions of sulfur dioxide and nitrogen oxide treated as precursors of acid rain to the establishment of fees designed to limit discharges of effluents into groundwater and, ultimately, marine systems.[8]

Incentive Systems

All these so-called incentive systems are designed to work by influencing calculations of costs and benefits on the part of those whose actions are expected to produce environmental side effects. Under such systems emitters of airborne pollutants are no longer allowed to use the atmosphere as an unregulated repository for wastes and, therefore, treat it as a free factor of production.[9] Those who discharge effluents into water systems will have an incentive to reduce their waste streams or treat them prior to discharging them into streams or lakes. What is more, emitters will have ongoing incentives to consider innovations that can lower the costs they incur in complying with the relevant rules. Those who find it easy to reduce their emissions may even be able to reap gains from trade by selling unneeded permits to others who find it harder to shift their actions in a cost-effective manner. If all goes well, society as a whole in contrast to a few members who can prove that they are victims will stand to benefit from the introduction of these incentive systems.

Not surprisingly, debates have emerged among advocates of incentive systems regarding the relative merits of different members of this family of strategies. The current debate about the pros and cons of what are known as cap-and-trade systems as opposed to tax systems as instruments for curbing emissions of greenhouse gases is instructive.[10] A cap-and-trade system works by imposing a ceiling on emissions and forces emitters to make investments in adjusting their actions to avoid exceeding the ceiling. A tax system, by contrast, imposes costs on emitters designed to induce them to alter production processes in ways that lead to reducing emissions by the desired amount. In principle either system can lead to the behavioral changes needed to fulfill socially determined goals, but the debate among proponents of the two approaches has become intense in a variety of settings.

Much of this debate turns on forecasts about how these systems would work in practice. Some question the efficacy of both approaches on the grounds that political pressures are likely to lead to the issuance of too many permits or the establishment of taxes that are too low to produce the desired changes. Others debate the costs of ensuring compliance with such arrangements in the sense of requiring emitters to surrender the requisite number of permits or of compelling actors to pay their taxes. Still others focus on conditions under which one system or the other is likely to prove particularly effective. For instance, in social settings in which collecting taxes is difficult and taking advantage of loopholes is relatively easy, emissions taxes may prove both costly to administer and ineffectual in altering behavior in the intended direction. A cap-and-trade system, however, may be vulnerable to political pressure to create a safety valve in the form of increasing the number of permits issued in response to an increase in the market price of permits. In every case there is a need to recognize the gap between the ideal and the actual in the operation of such systems and to avoid inappropriate comparisons between the ideal in one case and the actual in another.[11]

All this has led to a certain amount of skepticism about the superiority of incentive systems over traditional command-and-control systems.[12] In cases in which outright bans on certain kinds of environmental side effects (e.g., the adverse consequences of using drift nets in industrial fisheries) are in order, the differences between the two strategies may not be great. In every case much depends on how effective specific strategies are likely to prove under real-world conditions on a case-by-case basis. Beyond this lies the realm of equity and fairness, a matter that arises both in systems featuring victim's rights and those relying on rules and regulations.

New Directions

Recent thinking in this field has highlighted the drawbacks of all the mainstream approaches to dealing with unintended side effects. Court proceedings can drag on for years and produce unsatisfactory results. Command-and-control regulations are not only inefficient; they are also difficult to enforce and subject to distortion resulting from bureaucratic lethargy and corrupt practices. Incentives systems become focal points of political battles (e.g., contentious debates about cap-and-trade systems covering greenhouse gases) and often fail to solve problems even after they are put in place. These shortcomings have given rise to a lively debate about alternatives to the mainstream approaches together with some limited efforts to put new arrangements into practice.

Some analysts focus on the prospects for corporate social responsibility and even see private governance as a way to deal with unintended side effects that can cut down on the costs to society of institutional arthritis and corrupt practices associated with public governance. The idea here is that private actors—mainly corporations—will often find that they have an interest in environmental protection even in the absence of public regulations.[13] They can green existing production and distribution processes and save money by doing so, or they can develop more environmentally benign products and find markets for them. Others see opportunities featuring hybrid arrangements in which actors from both the public and the private sectors collaborate in efforts to reduce or eliminate harmful side effects. Such strategies may involve efforts on the part of government agencies to provide information that will allow private actors to alter production processes in such a way as to reduce side effects, measures that provide public support for new ventures featuring environmentally benign products (e.g., photovoltaic cells), or initiatives featuring the negotiation of consensual agreements between public and private actors as an alternative to the mandatory regulations that are the centerpiece of mainstream approaches.[14] At the international level there have been experiments with so-called Type II Partnerships, in which international agencies and corporations join forces to tackle challenges relating to sustainable development.

What are the prospects for these new approaches to coping with environmental side effects? There is no doubt that the mainstream approaches leave much to be desired, especially in dealing with large-scale problems like climate change and the loss of biological diversity. But experience with the new approaches is not yet sufficient to support clear-cut assessments of their effectiveness. So far much of the debate has focused on broad and often ideologically tinged assertions about the relative importance of market and government failures. A critical issue going forward will be to foster experiments with a variety of new approaches to coping with environmental side effects and to assess their results in different settings.

Environmental Justice

One of the most well-known findings emerging from thinking about environmental governance is known as the Coase Theorem.[15] Using an example in which stray cattle damage a neighbor's crops, this argument—developed initially by Ronald Coase—demonstrates that the allocation of resources will be the same whether the cattle owner is liable for the damages in question or the farmer must pay the owner to control his animals. The conclusion arises from the observation that the calculations of the cattle owner will be the same whether the farmer pays him to reduce the size of his herd or he reduces the size of his herd as a consequence of the cost arising from his obligation to compensate the farmer for the crop damage.[16] This is a powerful argument that has had a profound influence on thinking about ways to address matters of environmental protection, but it has nothing to say about matters of equity or fairness. Although the Coase Theorem is neutral regarding the desirability of making the cattle owner liable for the damages inflicted on the farmer, many—perhaps most—of those who think about such matters feel that considerations of equity or fairness demand some recognition that the farmer is a victim who deserves to receive some sort of compensation for the damages he suffers.

It turns out that this is one prominent example of a sizable class of issues relating to equity or fairness associated with efforts to cope with environmental side effects. For purposes of analysis it is helpful to differentiate among members of this class depending on whether they center on (i) damages that the actions of individual members of a group inflict on fellow members, (ii) the initial allocation of resources that become valuable as a consequence of innovative policies, or (iii) the incidence of benefits and costs arising from the actions of public authorities. To this collection of distributive issues we can add a concern for procedural justice or the extent to which the processes through which public decisions are made conform to community standards regarding fairness. In this section I focus on the distributive impacts of efforts to cope with environmental side effects, whereas in the next section I will discuss the procedural issues involved.

Environmental Damages

The issue of damages centers on the balance between the rights of property owners and the rights of others affected by the actions of owners. Advocates of property rights generally oppose the imposition of restrictions on the freedom to use property as the owner sees fit, arguing that actions of public authorities that impose regulatory restrictions constitute unjust reductions in the content of their bundles of rights and, in extreme cases, those restrictions amount to regulatory takings.[17] Supporters of those who suffer from the unintended consequences of the activities of property owners, by contrast, argue that compelling them to bear the costs of such actions is unfair and that, at a minimum, they should be compensated for the resultant damages. No simple procedure for balancing these conflicting claims yields results that are in some sense correct. But the way forward in most social settings is to introduce liability rules that spell out the circumstances under which victims can expect to receive compensation for damages inflicted on them.[18] A particularly sensitive issue in dealing with environmental side effects involves the idea of strict liability, the extent to which actors are culpable even when damages take the form of unintended consequences of their actions. It is easy to see that the content of liability rules will be sensitive to shifts in the balance of power in various social settings and that courts may arrive at disparate conclusions regarding the interpretation of liability rules as they seek to resolve disputes arising in specific situations. As the development of concepts like "toxic torts" makes clear, however, creating liability rules dealing with environmental side effects constitutes a front line in addressing issues of environmental justice.

Initial Allocation

In situations in which the actions of public authorities lead to the creation of quasi-markets, another set of issues relating to equity or fairness arises. Consider cases like the markets in permits for emissions of sulfur dioxide and nitrogen oxide in the United States or for emissions of greenhouse gases under the European Union's Emissions Trading Scheme (ETS). How should such permits be allocated at the outset, and what rules should govern trading among holders of such permits following the initial allocation?[19] There is an understandable tendency to grandfather such permits in the sense of allocating them to those emitting gases at the time the permits are created. But is this procedure, which produces what amounts to a windfall gain for emitters, equitable or fair? Why not auction the permits on an annual basis, thereby allocating them to those willing to pay the most for permits and creating a significant source of revenue available to public authorities to use for socially desirable purposes? Although this issue is often associated with domestic or regional policies, it also arises on a global scale. Once a global cap is established on emissions of greenhouse gases, would it not make sense to allocate the emissions permits globally on a per capita basis?[20] Among other things such a system could go far toward providing the funds developing countries or countries in the Global South need to adapt to climate change and even to make a transition toward a green economy. Politically, grandfathering in such situations constitutes the path of least resistance, especially in cases in which the influence of established industries is strong. Yet in addressing such matters ignoring the issues of equity lying close to the surface is difficult.

Other Public Actions

Other actions of public authorities also raise questions of justice relating to environmental side effects. Familiar examples include the location of waste treatment facilities, the construction of various forms of infrastructure, and the content of subsidies. In the United States, for example, there is a lively debate around the idea of NIMBYs (not in my backyard) and the assertion that public decisions about the location of dangerous or unattractive facilities reflect class and ethnic biases.[21] There are lively debates as well about intended or de facto subsidies in such forms as supplying water to farmers at below-market prices, subsidizing timber harvests on public lands, and providing tax breaks to producers of fossil fuels. All these arrangements raise fundamental issues of justice. Why should the poor bear the brunt of activities involving the treatment of hazardous wastes? Why should users of water for agricultural purposes receive public subsidies or producers of coal benefit from tax breaks? Anyone with even a superficial understanding of the role of organized interests in political processes will have no difficulty in explaining why such phenomena occur, but clearly, explaining such occurrences does not contribute in any way toward justifying them.

Good Governance

Beyond this lies a set of issues relating to what we can treat as good governance in efforts to come to terms with environmental side effects. We want to minimize harms such side effects cause and to do so in a manner that is compatible with reasonable standards of distributive justice. But we also want to achieve these goals through processes that conform as much as possible to a number of standards of what is increasingly treated as good governance.[22]

To begin with, this means arriving at public choices about matters like the content of liability rules, the allocation of permits, the location of waste treatment facilities, and so forth through processes that are transparent, participatory, unbiased, legitimate, and faithful to community standards of equity or fairness. These are demanding requirements, and it is to be expected that the gap between the ideal and the actual in this realm will be significant under real-world conditions. Nevertheless, there is no excuse for failing to make an effort to establish decision-making processes that take these normative considerations into account. In most instances the value of doing so is likely to be substantial on pragmatic as well as normative grounds. Decisions arrived at through transparent processes that stakeholders regard as legitimate and unbiased produce better results in terms of goal attainment than decisions made behind closed doors with little opportunity for participation on the part of stakeholders. This is especially true with regard to decisions that call for compliance with prohibitions or requirements on the part of large numbers of subjects on an ongoing basis. It is hard to achieve high levels of compliance with standards dealing with the treatment of toxic wastes or the emission of various air pollutants, for instance, in the absence of voluntary adjustments on the part of the great majority of subjects.

Another dimension of good governance, especially when it comes to administrative arrangements needed to move rules from paper to practice, involves avoiding or minimizing corruption. Corruption in the form of cronyism or crony capitalism is widespread in the administration of environmental regulations in developing countries. But what are known to those who study policy implementation as iron triangles—arrangements in which legislators, administrators, and lobbyists for specific industries develop mutually supportive relationships—are common in advanced industrial societies as well.[23] The perennial problems of reforming the rules governing the movement of key individuals from one of these roles to another and the rules governing campaign financing in modern political systems make it clear that corruption is not an issue that arises only in developing countries. The success of those favoring subsidies to producers of fossil fuels and opposing any meaningful restrictions on emissions of greenhouse gases in the United States is testimony to the influence of corrupt practices in modern democratic systems.[24]

Avoiding the paralysis associated with bureaucratization and institutional arthritis is another major component of good governance. Unlike corruption, which centers on manipulating political systems to promote the preferences of special interests, bureaucratization is a matter of increasingly severe inefficiency or sluggishness that arises in settings that are rule bound and not subject to real competition or incentives to pursue goals in an efficient manner.[25] There is no need to adopt the exaggerated claims of political conservatives regarding extreme government failure to recognize that institutional arthritis can become a source of major obstacles in efforts to cope with environmental side effects.[26] To take the case of the United States again, the process involved in moving policies from paper to practice through the promulgation of regulations can take years. The administrative capacity needed to apply the regulations to specific cases is often lacking. Efforts to enforce the regulations through the use of legal procedures are apt to be minimal, become enmeshed in endless appeals, and eventuate in modest fines even when final judgments are rendered. Ironically, environmental advocates are sometimes able to make good use of these features of the system to promote their own causes by obstructing processes involving the production of environmental-impact assessments and using the courts to seek injunctive relief until all the challenges to proposed initiatives likely to have significant environmental impacts are finally resolved. Whether this is a good thing or a bad thing naturally depends on the values one brings to assessing the performance of governance systems, but it is undeniable that such processes impose high costs (often characterized as transaction costs) on society. This is a matter of increasing concern in an era in which rising budget deficits have become an issue of overriding importance in public policy arenas.

Conclusion

The growth of human populations, affluence, and technological capacity has increased interdependencies at all levels.[27] I address this phenomenon in some detail in later chapters, focusing on the implications of what has become known as the Great Acceleration. For now it is enough to observe that this development is responsible for a dramatic rise in the frequency and intensity of environmental side effects. Whereas small and widely dispersed bands of hunter-gatherers could pursue their own livelihoods in a manner that did not greatly affect the welfare of others, even modest actions in highly interdependent systems can produce side effects that impinge significantly on the welfare of others. Today, these side effects occur on a large and sometimes global scale in contrast to the local impacts more common in the past. Emissions of greenhouse gases anywhere, for instance, can prove detrimental to the well-being of those living anywhere on the planet. Ironically, those whose actions are least significant as drivers of climate change feel the earliest and (probably) the most severe of these environmental side effects.

This means that traditional methods for coming to terms with environmental side effects (e.g., the development of the nuisance doctrine in common law systems) are no longer sufficient as strategies for addressing the resultant problems. Regulatory systems, with all their flaws and limitations, must become an increasingly important element in the tool kit available for dealing with such matters, and the resultant arrangements must be adapted for use in global settings where there is no government in the usual sense of the term. Experiments with new approaches that feature ideas like corporate social responsibility are in order. In this regard the protracted debates going on now about the relative merits of alternative policy instruments available to deal with problems like climate change are somewhat unsettling, especially for those who believe that decisive actions to address such problems are needed immediately.[28] Even so, there is a sense in which these debates constitute signs of vitality in efforts to come up with innovative strategies that will prove effective in addressing environmental side effects that are unprecedented in terms of both scope and complexity.

CHAPTER THREE
ECOSYSTEM SERVICES

THINKING IN SYSTEMS

Humans eat fish as a source of protein, convert trees into a variety of wood products, use soil and water to grow crops, transform hydrocarbons into sources of energy, and make use of hard-rock minerals in a range of technological applications. These commodities are all forms of "natural capital" produced by nature and available for consumption to enhance individual well-being and social welfare. Understandable as this perspective on natural capital is under a variety of conditions, however, three linked developments unfolding over the last several decades have drawn attention to the inadequacy of this commoditization paradigm as the dominant mode of thinking about the use of natural capital.

As pressures from efforts to meet the growing demand for material goods have risen, we have become increasingly aware of the ecological consequences of using natural resources to satisfy the demand for material goods and services. Once a coastal wetland is drained to expand the land base for urban development, for instance, it can no longer perform a variety of ecological functions, including providing a nursery for marine organisms and serving as a filtration system to handle various types of wastes. Land cleared for agricultural uses is no longer available to maintain biological diversity by providing habitat for forest-based species. A second development centers on the growth of interest in amenities as opposed to commodities on the part of humans whose material needs are largely satisfied. The value of setting aside undeveloped lands to be enjoyed as parks and even wilderness areas, thereby making them unavailable for consumptive uses, has risen steadily among affluent people who find pleasure in inspiring scenery and contact with nature. Charismatic megafauna, such as elephants and whales, are now valued by many who enjoy seeing them in the wild or just knowing that they exist, giving rise to interests that conflict with the interests of those who regard these animals as sources of commodities (e.g., elephant ivory, whale oil) or as pests who interfere with their efforts to make a living (e.g., elephants that damage crops in southern Africa).

Overarching these developments is the rise of new analytic constructs or paradigms emphasizing the central role of complex and dynamic systems that have revolutionized our understanding of human-environment relations.[1] We have become aware of the role of human actions in the degradation of land and resultant losses of biodiversity, the destruction of benthic communities and the consequent damage to large marine ecosystems, and the changing composition of the Earth's atmosphere and its impacts on the planet's climate system. The lack of awareness or concern regarding such matters did not pose a serious threat to complex ecosystems so long as human populations remained small and the capacity of humans to intervene in biophysical systems was limited.[2] But we can no longer afford the luxury of ignoring these issues without consequences. Human actions have become powerful driving forces that affect the Earth System at every level.[3]

This chapter explores this topic through an examination of the development of the concept of ecosystem services and its implications for environmental governance. The next two sections focus on the nature of ecosystem services and the various attempts that have been made to calculate the contribution these services make to human well-being and social welfare. The following section provides an account of the reasons why ecosystem services are often undervalued or simply ignored in decision making on the part of individuals who consume natural capital in various forms as well as policy-makers responsible for promoting social welfare. This sets the stage for an analysis of alternative strategies for conserving ecosystem services or, more precisely, for including the value of ecosystem services in making decisions about the use of natural capital. Here, we are still in the realm of what I call simple environmental governance. But as thinking in systems draws our attention to linkages among issue areas and across levels of biophysical and socioeconomic structures, the need for new ways of addressing challenges of environmental governance begins to come into focus.

What Are Ecosystem Services?

Those who have led the way in drawing attention to ecosystem services have offered a number of ways of thinking about the content of this new concept. Gretchen Daily speaks of ecosystem services as "the conditions and processes through which natural ecosystems . . . sustain and fulfill human life."[4] Robert Costanza and his colleagues refer to "Ecosystem goods (such as food) and services (such as waste assimilation) [as] the benefits human populations derive, directly or indirectly, from ecosystem functions."[5] The Millennium Ecosystem Assessment (MEA), whose 2005 report *Ecosystems and Human Well-Being* has played a influential role in drawing the concept of ecosystem services to the attention of policy-makers and members of the attentive public, builds on these definitions to encompass goods and services that are valued for both consumptive and non-consumptive purposes and that may or may not require human action to realize their potential.[6] What unifies all these perspectives is a focus on human well-being and social welfare. Nature supplies ecosystem services—hence the frequent references to natural capital in thinking about them. They are valuable to the extent that they contribute to the quality of human lives.

A concrete example may help to convey some sense of the range of values that the idea of ecosystem services encompasses. Consider the contributions of a forest to human well-being and social welfare.[7] A (undoubtedly partial) listing of these contributions includes:

- wood products, such as building materials, pulp, and fuelwood;
- food products, such as nuts and mushrooms;
- household goods, such as wooden bowls and implements;
- materials for farm implements and fishing boats;
- habitat for wildlife leading to the protection of biodiversity;
- control of erosion;
- purification of wastes;
- fixing of carbon dioxide as a contribution to climate stability;
- sources of traditional medicines;
- educational opportunities;
- recreational opportunities in such forms as walking, hiking, and skiing;
- scenic panoramas; and
- spiritual experiences.

Several observations regarding this listing of values stand out and deserve comment immediately. Some of these values are non-rival; a forest can provide habitat for wildlife, fix carbon, control erosion, purify wastes, and offer opportunities for recreation at the same time. But others are rival in the sense that one use precludes or diminishes other uses; trees cut for building materials or for use in making farm implements can no longer fix carbon, provide recreational opportunities, or form part of a scenic panorama. However, properly managed harvesting of trees can provide habitat for a different array of wildlife and may fix carbon at a faster pace as soon as new growth gets started. The list of uses also serves to clarify the issue of direct and indirect contributions to human well-being. Forests in their natural state can provide food products, habitat for wildlife, and recreational opportunities on a direct basis. But the provision of wood products normally requires effort in the form of harvesting, milling, and marketing to make these products valuable to human users. Beyond this lies the question of sustainability. It is common to speak of sustainable yields as a goal in discussions of forest management; this idea is straightforward, at least in conceptual terms. But it is another and more complex matter to grasp the meaning of sustainability in thinking about the entire suite of values that are or can be derived from human interactions with forests.

In an effort to impose some order on the analysis of ecosystem services the MEA adopted a practice of classifying services along functional lines using categories of provisioning, regulating, cultural, and supporting services (see figure 3.1).[8] Provisioning services are products like food, fuelwood, and genetic resources. Regulating services encompass values like water purification, disease control, and climate stabilization. Cultural services include education, recreation, and spiritual experiences. Supporting services cut across all

Figure 3.1 Types of Ecosystem Services

ECOSYSTEM SERVICES

Provisioning
- FOOD
- FRESH WATER
- WOOD AND FIBER
- FUEL
- ...

Supporting
- NUTRIENT CYCLING
- SOIL FORMATION
- PRIMARY PRODUCTION
- ...

Regulating
- CLIMATE REGULATION
- FLOOD REGULATION
- DISEASE REGULATION
- WATER PURIFICATION
- ...

Cultural
- AESTHETIC
- SPIRITUAL
- EDUCATIONAL
- RECREATIONAL
- ...

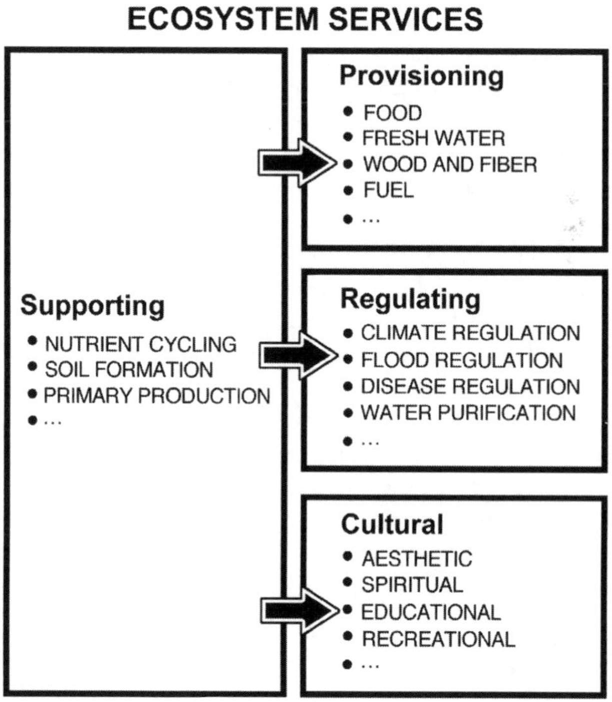

After Millennium Ecosystem Assessment.

the other categories, supplying things like soil formation and nutrient cycling. There is nothing sacred about this functional classification. As I argue in a later section of this chapter, strategies for maximizing the contributions of ecosystem services to human well-being and social welfare do not divide neatly along the lines of this classification. Nevertheless, the MEA's approach fills an important niche in thinking about ecosystem services, has been widely disseminated, and is certainly worth bearing in mind as we think about issues of governance associated with ecosystem services.

The Value of Ecosystem Services

What is the value of ecosystem services? In some cases the answer to this question is relatively straightforward. So long as we assume that markets are more or less competitive and more or less comparable in various parts of the world, we can make estimates of the value of building materials and pulpwood by multiplying quantities times market prices, aggregating the result to arrive at national totals and adjusting for purchasing power parity to come up with a global figure. In other cases the situation is far more complex. For example, how should we calculate the roles that forests play in providing habitat for numerous species, controlling soil erosion, and fixing carbon? And what about the aesthetic and inspirational values that people derive from experiencing an intact old-growth forest (e.g., a stand of redwoods)? Fundamentally, there are two distinct lines of attack in efforts to answer questions of this sort. One is essentially utilitarian in the sense that it seeks ways to compute values for the full range of ecosystem services that can be expressed in monetary terms. The other, based largely on a sense that the utilitarian approach is inadequate or even misleading, seeks to bring alternative normative perspectives to bear on the problem of valuing ecosystem services.

Approaches to Valuation

Those adopting a utilitarian perspective have worked hard not only to address distortions attributable to market imperfections but also and especially to develop methods for attaching values to ecosystem services for which market prices are nonexistent.[9] This has resulted in a proliferation of (at best partial) approaches to valuation, including estimates of replacement costs, assessments of how much people are willing to pay for a home with a view in contrast to one without a view, and what is known as contingent valuation, in which people are given various scenarios and asked about their willingness to pay for alternatives that vary in terms of the ecosystem services they include.[10] To put it mildly, these procedures leave a lot to be desired as methods for arriving at realistic estimates of the value of ecosystem services. Their virtue, according to analysts like Costanza, who have made sustained efforts to measure the value of ecosystem services, is that they draw attention to the tremendous value of these services, a value that is often overlooked by those who take the existence of ecosystem services for granted and assume that they will always be available. Costanza and his colleagues have calculated the value of ecosystem services (most of which is outside the market) as of 1997 "to be in the range of US$16–54 trillion . . . per year, with an average of US$33 trillion per year."[11] The magnitude of this figure acquires particular significance in light of the observation that the "Global gross national product total is around US$18 trillion per year."[12] On this account the value to human beings of the Earth's natural capital is immense, a conclusion that demonstrates the importance of protecting natural capital or at least recognizing the cost to society of any actions that lead to the consumption or degradation of this capital.

The other approach, which is not necessarily at odds with the utilitarian approach, seeks to develop alternative ways to think about the value of ecosystem services. Some of the resultant procedures seek to find other currencies in terms of which to express the value of ecosystem services. A prominent example features the articulation of the principle that people have a (human) right to enjoy the provisioning and cultural services of nature and makes the case that rights trump simple utilitarian calculations.[13] In other words, people should not be deprived of key ecosystem services, regardless of the benefits that others may derive from the exploitation of these services. Other, more radical, arguments raise questions about the anthropocentric character of much of the debate about ecosystem services. What is the ethical or moral justification of modes of thought that are based squarely on the premise that ecosystem services are valuable primarily or even exclusively to the extent that they contribute to individual well-being and social welfare?[14] There is a longstanding tradition in many indigenous cultures, for instance, that focuses on the role of humans as stewards of the Earth rather than simply beneficiaries of ecosystem services. On this account the members of each generation have an obligation to pass the Earth on to the next generation in a condition that is as good or better than the condition in which they received it from the preceding generation.[15] These nonutilitarian approaches to thinking about the value of ecosystem services are not as neat or as crisp as calculations of benefits and costs appear to be. Yet a raft of analytical and empirical problems lurks just beneath the surface of utilitarian calculations regarding the value of ecosystem services. And the nonutilitarian approaches tap into a deep sense in the thinking of many people that it is inappropriate to reduce the value of ecosystems services and natural capital more generally to conventional calculations of benefits and costs.

Resolving Conflicts

These distinct approaches to valuation sometimes produce conflicting results along with heated debates between the proponents of one or the other. How can we compare the market value of wood products, for example, with the aesthetic, educational, and inspirational experiences many people derive from intact forests much less with the view that we should approach such questions from a nonanthropocentric perspective? Leaving these hard-to-resolve differences aside for the moment, it is worth pointing out that there is a good deal of overlap in the take-home messages that these alternative approaches yield. However we think about them, ecosystem services are immensely valuable, often taken for granted, and in need of much more attention as we move deeper into an era of human-dominated ecosystems. What is required at this stage is a focused assessment of the needs for governance growing out of these propositions and of the options for meeting these needs.

Governance Challenges

Some decisions about the use of ecosystem services—especially those framed in terms of natural capital—seem perfectly reasonable. Owners of well-managed forests, for example, are cognizant of the importance of sustainability; they endeavor to manage their resources in a manner that produces sustainable yields over long periods of time. Farmers generally recognize the desirability of growing crops on a sustainable basis; they rotate crops and allow land to lie fallow from time to time as a means of maintaining the productivity of their farming operations. Nevertheless, there is no denying the pervasiveness of practices that fail to take into account the value to society of many ecosystem services and that lead to situations in which many of these services are overused or under-protected. Three differentiable—albeit related—problems pose challenges for governance in this realm: (i) the degradation and even destruction of ecosystem services that are not properly valued, (ii) underinvestment in ecosystem services that are valuable from a societal perspective, and (iii) inappropriate trade-offs between or among rival ecosystems services.

Degradation of Ecosystem Services

Appropriators who are able to use ecosystem services free of charge are apt to overuse them or to fail to take them into account in calculating the benefits and costs of the options available to them. The use of the atmosphere as a repository for wastes, such as sulfur dioxide and carbon dioxide, presents a dramatic case in point. So long as there are no rules governing such practices, decision-makers will treat the atmosphere as a free good in making their calculations; their natural inclination will be to consume as much of this good as possible, thereby freeing resources to pay for other factors of production (e.g., capital, labor, technology) that are not free. Similarly, actors who perceive that they can simply move on from one source of natural capital to another are apt to ignore the degradation or destruction of ecosystem services associated with their actions. This is the problem that a number of analysts have described in terms of the concept of roving bandits.[16] An actor who believes that it is possible to move on from one location to the next will not experience incentives to conserve natural capital. So long as new grazing lands are readily available to replace those that have been degraded or exhausted or new forests are available to replace those that have been clear-cut or treated in an unsustainable manner, for instance, users will have little incentive to think about the degradation of ecosystem services resulting from their actions. Yet there is no escaping the fact that such actions are apt to leave a trail of destruction with regard to ecosystem services, ranging from erosion control to the protection of habitat and on to the use of such resources on the part of those who are interested in recreational or aesthetic experiences.

Underinvestment

To this problem of overuse we must add the propensity of individual actors to underinvest in the protection or development of ecosystem services. Relatively modest investments may suffice to ensure that forested land contributes to erosion control, wetlands are able to purify water, or open land plays a role in the survival of species. But so long as these ecosystem services produce no income for those making decisions affecting their use, there will be no incentive to pay attention to them in making choices about the use of natural capital. Analysts have shown repeatedly that actions like avoiding land degradation, protecting wetlands, preserving mangrove forests, and so forth can produce benefits to society that far outweigh the benefits that individuals derive from actions that degrade or destroy these ecosystems. But there is no reason for individuals to pay attention to such calculations, so long as actions designed to maintain the services derived from these ecosystems do not produce benefits for them. The problem here is that there is a disjunction between the benefits associated with ecosystem services accruing to the individual and the benefits accruing to society. Whenever this is the case, the idea that individuals can take actions that are good for society while doing well themselves is no longer tenable.[17]

Inappropriate Trade-offs

Where ecosystem services are rival in the sense that taking advantage of one service is costly in terms of damage to others, individual decision-makers are apt to make trade-offs among the relevant values that, from a societal point of view, are inappropriate. Such problems are particularly prominent in cases in which consumptive uses have consequences that are destructive from the perspective of those interested in nonconsumptive uses. Once again, the case of the forest is illustrative.[18] The attractions of clear-cutting or even conversion into agricultural land are often substantial from the point of view of private owners who think exclusively about their own well-being and have little incentive to take the broader consequences of their actions into account. In the absence of interventions on the part of society, in other words, these owners will have little reason to think about losses of recreational opportunities, aesthetic enjoyment, or spiritual experiences arising from the decisions they make about clear-cutting or converting land for agricultural purposes. When one choice produces a tangible income stream and the other enhances social welfare without producing rewards in terms of individual well-being, the behavior of the individual actor is predictable. So long as he acts in a manner that is roughly rational and self-interested, he will opt for the tangible income stream every time. Here too the tension between individual well-being and social welfare is often dramatic.

Strategies for Protecting Ecosystem Services

What options are available to those desiring to address these governance challenges relating to ecosystem services? As in the cases of collective-action problems and problems involving environmental side effects, the challenges here center on mismatches between the incentives of individuals and the interests of society. Individuals desiring to maximize payoffs to themselves often have good reasons to overuse ecosystem services, underinvest in their protection or development, make choices that discount the future heavily, and favor trade-offs that seem inappropriate from a societal perspective. Accordingly, efforts to protect ecosystem services or use them sustainably must address these mismatches, in the process finding ways to alter individuals' behavior. The strategies available for pursuing this goal resemble those discussed in the preceding chapters. But now there is a need to direct attention to complex socioecological systems rather than individual natural resources or specific harms.[19] Three families of strategies are worthy of consideration in this context. One, we can appeal to social practices and ethical principles that induce individuals to lengthen their time horizons and pay attention to social welfare rather than focusing on immediate benefits to themselves in using ecosystem services. Two, we can take steps to alter the incentives or the calculations actors make regarding the benefits and costs associated with the use of ecosystem services. Or, finally, we can turn to some public authority to articulate rules and regulations about such matters and devise compliance mechanisms that will prove effective in influencing the behavior of (most of) those whose actions make a difference in terms of the fate of ecosystem services.

Social Practices and Ethical Principles

Social practices are well-defined patterns of behavior reflecting knowledge accumulated over time and often cast in the form of norms or ethical principles. Such practices are generally rooted in experiential knowledge about sustainability in hunting and gathering, cultivating crops, or managing forests.[20] They are often framed as spiritual or religious injunctions, a feature that can play a critical role in inducing individuals to comply with them. Are practices of this sort mainly of interest to anthropologists and ethnographers, or are they relevant in one form or another to contemporary settings, in which issues involving sustainable uses of ecosystem services now arise at regional and even global scales? Normative precepts like those embedded in Aldo Leopold's "land ethic" come into focus in this context. Leopold was not opposed to consumptive uses of natural resources; trained as a forester and comfortable with hunting wild animals, he spent most of his career working on issues involving sustainable uses of natural resources. In the process he came to the conclusion that we need a third system of ethics to supplement existing ethical systems that guide the actions of individuals and the interactions between or among individuals. He called this third system the land ethic and placed at its core the principle that a "thing is right when it tends to preserve the integrity, stability, and beauty of the biotic community."[21] There is no basis for asserting that a land ethic has taken root in society at large and can be counted on to protect ecosystem services on a large scale today, yet it is important to recognize that Leopold and others like him, who have directed attention to ethical precepts as guides to behavior, have hit on a critical point. There is much to be said for the proposition that some such foundation—in contrast to purely utilitarian calculations of benefits and costs—is critical in guiding the course of human-environment relations. This observation is especially relevant to situations involving large and complex biophysical systems and human actions whose impacts will be felt on time scales of decades to centuries in contrast to months and years.

Incentive Mechanisms

Nonetheless, these observations do not diminish the importance of a second family of strategies featuring the use of incentive systems designed to protect ecosystem services. The basic idea here, which often involves some sort of privatization, centers on measures that provide individuals with reasons to conserve ecosystem services. If the owner of a forest can introduce exclusion mechanisms that make it possible to collect fees from those who want to gather mushrooms or nuts or to use the forest for recreational purposes, for example, it may benefit him to refrain from harvesting wood products or to do so on a basis that does not interfere with these nonconsumptive uses. Similarly, if society is willing to compensate the owner of the forest for maintaining it in a state that contributes to preventing large-scale erosion or provides habitat for species that society wants to protect, the owner may alter his actions in ways that favor nonconsumptive ecosystem services. Of course, measures of this sort depend both on the feasibility of creating exclusion mechanisms that are effective and affordable and on the willingness of society to act in ways that make a difference to the incentives of those who own or at least hold use and exclusion rights relating to the relevant biophysical systems. These are critical conditions that may be difficult or impossible to meet in a wide range of settings, but they are not impossible to meet. Consider cases, for example, in which conservation organizations (e.g., The Nature Conservancy) pay landowners to relinquish development rights to their holdings, or public authorities (e.g., state governments) provide landowners with tax breaks if they agree to restrictions on the development of their holdings.[22] In cases in which these incentive mechanisms are joined together with normative or ethical principles in owners' minds, the result may be the protection of nonconsumptive ecosystem services on a relatively large scale.

Appeals to Public Authority

In the final analysis, however, protecting ecosystem services is apt to require action on the part of some public authority (e.g., a national government). Broadly speaking, a public authority may address these concerns in two—by no means mutually exclusive—ways. It can make decisions about uses of publicly owned lands and natural resources (i.e., the public domain) or areas like watersheds and airsheds over which it can exercise authority as a matter of public trust.[23] Or the authority can adopt rules and promulgate the regulations necessary to implement them relating to the actions of private owners in a variety of settings. Both options are important and may play critical roles in efforts to protect or sustain ecosystem services.

Most governments own a sizable portion of the land base in areas over which they exercise authority. Even in the United States the homeland of private property and free enterprise, the federal government owns about a third of the country's land.[24] Subnational governments own an additional chunk of the total. In such cases the government can take steps to protect ecosystem services of various kinds associated with the public domain. It can, for example, designate some land to be used for purposes of recreation (e.g., national parks) or for the protection of wildlife (e.g., national wildlife refuges), even as it takes steps to open other parts of the public domain for consumptive uses (e.g., harvesting of wood products in national forests) or pursues policies leading to transfers of ownership from the public domain to private ownership (e.g., the claim/patent system governing mining on public lands in the United States). In recent decades the idea of wilderness areas (i.e., lands and associated ecosystems largely untouched by any consumptive uses) has emerged as a significant force leading to decisions that call for setting aside relatively large chunks of the public domain for nonconsumptive purposes, like providing habitat for wildlife, study areas for scientists, and stirring scenery of interest even to those who are able to enjoy it only through photographs or films.[25]

Although river systems and coastal waters are not part of the public domain in formal terms, governments in many places have acquired authority to manage them through extensions of what is known as the public trust doctrine. This does not provide any assurance that the management of these forms of natural capital will favor nonconsumptive uses. Governments regularly act to dam rivers so as to create irrigation systems and generate hydropower, support commercial fisheries in coastal waters, and encourage the search for oil and gas in offshore areas. Nonetheless, the development of the idea of a public trust has provided a point of departure for those who espouse the application of systems thinking to managing watersheds, estuaries, and coastal waters. In the United States this has resulted in designating some watersheds as wild and scenic rivers and establishing marine protected areas. Although thinking about the ecosystem services airsheds provide is less advanced, there is clearly room for public policies designed to protect these resources. The imposition of regulations intended to curb emissions of sulfur dioxide from coal-fired power plants, the principal precursor of acid rain, illustrates the scope for developing public policy in this realm.[26] Those who advocate policies designed to curb emissions of greenhouse gases are pushing for introducing regulations designed to terminate the use of airsheds as repositories for wastes treated as free services.

The other option centers on the efforts of public authorities to regulate behavior on the part of individual actors—including corporations as well as private citizens—that affects the sustainability of ecosystem services. This option covers a diverse collection of policies, ranging from zoning ordinances regulating the actions of homeowners through initiatives aimed at protecting wetlands and barrier beaches and on to actions designed to preserve endangered species. As might be expected, such efforts are highly sensitive politically, especially in countries like the United States, where the rights of private owners and the freedom of individuals to do as they please with their property are sacrosanct. The result is a battle that seesaws back and forth between those who oppose such policies on the grounds that they amount to regulatory takings or violations of the rights of landowners and those who argue that protecting ecosystem services is a necessary—though not sufficient—condition for sustainability in human-environment relations in the foreseeable future.

Public policies in the form of subsidies and taxes also play a role in efforts to avoid or mitigate commoditizing ecosystem services. In a good many cases the net effect of these policies is actually the reverse. Subsidies and tax breaks granted to producers and consumers of fossil fuels provide dramatic examples, but other cases featuring direct or de facto subsidies going to industrial-scale agriculture and harvesters of wood products are easy to identify. Even so, policies featuring taxes and subsidies are becoming increasingly valuable as tools available to those concerned with sustainability in human-environment relations. Prominent examples include support for developers of wind and solar power as well as tax incentives for individuals and businesses willing to take the initiative to make their homes and businesses more climate friendly. When the balance of such policies will tip toward supporting nonconsumptive ecosystem services is a complex matter that is sensitive to broader political trends that have little to do with ecosystem services themselves (e.g., the rise of the Tea Party in the United States). But there is no doubt that public authorities are in a position to provide leadership in efforts to protect ecosystem services when the general public begins to take an interest in such matters.

Conclusion

What are the prospects that societies will move toward adopting principles and practices under which nonconsumptive ecosystem services, such as providing opportunities for spiritual growth, contributing to the protection of biological diversity, and storing carbon as a way to mitigate climate change, become prominent considerations? At one level this is a matter of avoiding dilemmas of collective action and coping with environmental side effects on a particularly large scale. But there is more to it than this. The problem here is to direct attention to the range and importance of the services that ecosystems provide over and above the traditional commodities, such as soil and water to grow crops, trees that can be turned into wood products, and minerals that have a variety of industrial uses. Whether or not it makes sense to endeavor to attach dollar values to such services is debatable. But it is clearly essential to draw citizens' attention to the magnitude of the values at stake and the fact that there are no substitutes for many of these services, including clean air and a benign climate system.

Two factors offer some hope for progressive developments in this realm. First and arguably foremost is the development of systems thinking and the recognition that human actions are now important driving forces at a global scale. The result is the rise of what we now think of as Earth System Science.[27] I will come back to this development in a later chapter. For now, however, it is enough to note that we are developing intellectual capital of a sort that is essential to grasping the critical role of natural capital as a source of individual well-being and social welfare. The other factor centers on the rise of values that direct attention to amenities and various nonconsumptive uses of resources in contrast to commodities. Understandably, the materialistic lifestyles that those who reside in advanced industrial societies enjoy attract many consumers in developing countries. Yet the fact that these lifestyles are not sustainable on a global and long-term basis is becoming apparent to thoughtful observers every-where. Although this does not guarantee that a shift in values needed to redefine the idea of a good life will occur on a widespread basis, it is a step in the right direction.

Part II

Complex Environmental Governance

CHAPTER FOUR
HORIZONTAL INTERPLAY

DEALING WITH BROADER CONSEQUENCES

The preceding chapters focus, for the most part, on what I call simple environmental governance. They address well-defined issue areas (e.g., commercial fishing, timber harvesting, oil and gas development, hard-rock mining, management of toxic wastes, regulation of air pollutants) and focus on the performance of more or less self-contained regimes established to address these concerns one at a time. The discussion in chapter 3 dealing with ecosystem services began to move beyond these somewhat restrictive confines, but this was due mainly to the fact that the same biophysical systems contribute to individual well-being and social welfare in a number of ways rather than to the establishment of two or more distinct environmental regimes governing human actions pertaining to these systems.

The focus on self-contained regimes is valuable as a means of exploring the character of issues like the tragedy of the commons, the free-rider problem, and the challenge of coping with environmental side effects. But now it is time to move on toward an account of environmental governance systems as they operate under real-world conditions. The first major step in this direction is to come to grips with the fact that governance systems dealing with a variety of concerns at the same level of social organization frequently interact with one another. At the national level, for instance, distinct regimes dealing with commercial fishing, recreational fishing, shipping, swimming and boating, offshore oil and gas development, seabed mining, coastal wetland protection, hazardous waste disposal, marine pollution, onshore development affecting coastal waters, and so forth interact with one another in more or less significant ways.[1] Internationally, regimes dealing with fishing, shipping, deep seabed mining, marine pollution, and research interact not only with one another but also with national regimes applicable within the Exclusive Economic Zones of coastal states. To create and administer effective governance systems under these conditions it is not enough to devise functionally specific regimes designed to operate effectively on a self-contained basis. Rather, successful regimes need to manage tensions arising from institutional interplay and even take advantage of opportunities for synergistic interactions with neighboring regimes.

This chapter addresses the theme of institutional interplay in three steps. The first section sets the stage. It introduces concepts that are useful in characterizing the landscape of interplay between and among governance systems and identifies several types of interplay that resemble one another in some ways but that deserve separate treatment in an effort to understand this phenomenon. The next section addresses what we can think of as the politics of interplay. It begins with the observation that self-interested actors will be alert to ways to advance their own causes in conjunction with institutional interplay and explores the strategies they adopt in both the formation of environmental regimes and the administration of these arrangements following their creation. The final substantive section turns to what analysts call interplay management. It starts from the observation that much of the interest in interactions between distinct regimes flows from a concern that such interactions may generate harmful consequences with regard to the effectiveness of one or more of the regimes involved. The central question here has to do with strategies or families of strategies available to those responsible for designing or administering regimes and desiring to maximize the ratio of positive to negative interactions. The objective is not only to identify differentiable strategies but also to analyze the circumstances under which individual strategies are likely to work best. The take-home message is one of cautious optimism: although institutional interplay can become a source of problems, alert actors can often minimize harmful consequences and promote positive interactions.[2] Under the right circumstances interplay among regimes addressing different issues can produce synergy.

The Landscape of Institutional Interplay

The first step in describing the landscape of institutional interplay is to draw a distinction between horizontal interactions and vertical interactions.[3] Horizontal interactions are those that take place at the same level of social organization from local or regional interactions on up to national interactions and international or global interactions. Examples at each level are easy to identify. At the local level zoning ordinances designed to eliminate or minimize environmental side effects associated with development often come into conflict with the rights of owners of private property. National regimes created to provide protection for endangered species can generate tensions not only with the property rights of private owners but also with the management regimes created to address mainstream uses of the public domain, such as timber harvesting or hard-rock mining. International regimes, like the arrangement dealing with trade in endangered species of wild fauna and flora, can interfere with the normal application of the principles of the regime governing international trade.

Vertical interplay, by contrast, occurs when regimes interact across levels of social organization. Whereas interactions between the international regimes dealing with climate and biological diversity are horizontal in nature, interactions between these international regimes and the regimes dealing with the same or similar issues at the national level, for example, give rise to vertical interplay. Horizontal and vertical interplay can and often do occur at the same time, leading to increasingly complex systems of environmental governance. For purposes of analysis, however, I address the two types of interplay separately. This chapter focuses on cases of horizontal interplay, leaving an examination of vertical interplay to the next chapter. Throughout, however, it will be useful to bear in mind the prospect of links between horizontal and vertical interplay.

Negative and Positive Consequences

Next is the distinction, alluded to in the introduction to this chapter, between cases of institutional interplay that generate negative consequences and those that yield positive results. The prospects for negative interactions loom large in the thinking of many observers, especially in settings where the density of governance systems is great and growing.[4] At the international level many worry about the prospects that environmental regimes that have provisions relating to trade (e.g., the regimes dealing with transboundary movements of hazardous wastes, trade in endangered species of fauna and flora, and ozone depleting substances) will fall afoul of key elements of the global regime dealing with trade in goods and services. Because the trade regime is highly developed and deeply entrenched, the usual fear is that the effectiveness of the environmental regimes will suffer as a consequence of these overlaps. Similar issues arise at other levels of social organization. The spotted owl controversy in the United States, in which an effort to protect an endangered species threatened to undermine the regime governing the harvest of timber on public lands in the Pacific Northwest, is a dramatic but by no means unusual example.

Nevertheless, cases of positive interaction are not hard to find. A striking illustration involves interaction between the Kyoto Protocol in the regime dealing with emissions of greenhouse gases and the Montreal Protocol in the regime designed to protect the stratospheric ozone layer. Because some of the chemicals regulated under the Montreal Protocol are also greenhouse gases, the success of this regime in protecting the ozone layer generates side effects that are beneficial with regard to addressing the problem of climate change. As figure 4.1 demonstrates, the Montreal Protocol has played a far more important role to date in reducing emissions of greenhouse gases than the Kyoto Protocol has.[5] Similar examples of synergistic interaction occur at other levels of social interaction. A prominent

Figure 4.1 Climate Protection from the Montreal Protocol and Kyoto Protocol

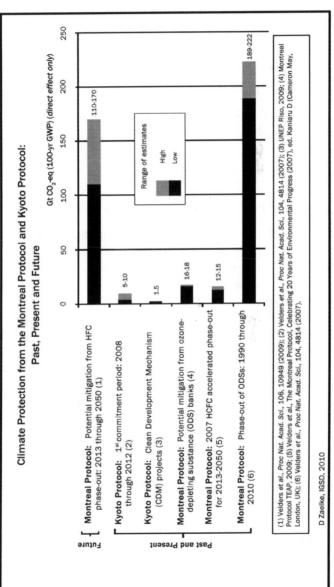

Climate Protection from the Montreal Protocol and Kyoto Protocol: Past, Present and Future

Gt CO$_2$-eq (100-yr GWP) *(direct effect only)*

Future

Montreal Protocol: Potential mitigation from HFC phase-out: 2013 through 2050 (1) — 110-170

Past and Present

Kyoto Protocol: 1st commitment period: 2008 through 2012 (2) — 5-10

Kyoto Protocol: Clean Development Mechanism (CDM) projects (3) — 1.5

Montreal Protocol: Potential mitigation from ozone-depleting substance (ODS) banks (4) — 16-18

Montreal Protocol: 2007 HCFC accelerated phase-out for 2013-2050 (5) — 12-15

Montreal Protocol: Phase-out of ODSs: 1990 through 2010 (6) — 189-222

Range of estimates
High
Low

(1) Velders et al., Proc Nat. Acad. Sci., 106, 10949 (2009); (2) Velders et al., Proc Nat. Acad. Sci., 104, 4814 (2007); (3) UNEP Riso, 2009; (4) Montreal Protocol TEAP, 2009; (5) Velders et al., The Montreal Protocol, Celebrating 20 Years of Environmental Progress (2007), ed. Kaniaru D (Cameron May, London, UK); (6) Velders et al., Proc Nat. Acad. Sci., 104, 4814 (2007).

D Zaelke, IGSD, 2010

After Institute on Governance for Sustainable Development. Reprinted with permission.

case arises from the overlay of wilderness status on lands that are already managed as part of the system of fish and wildlife refuges in the United States. The regime for wilderness areas constitutes a distinct system; areas included in the system of fish and wildlife refuges may or may not be designated as wilderness. But when they are, the provisions governing human activities in wilderness areas are likely to prove beneficial with regard to sustaining populations of fish and wildlife even as they restrict or prohibit various familiar activities. This explains why decisions to add a wilderness overlay to areas included in refuges (e.g., the Arctic National Wildlife Refuge in Alaska) can become matters of intense political controversy.

Interplay Within and Between Issue Domains

As the examples introduced in the preceding paragraphs suggest, institutional interplay can involve regimes operating in the same issue domain (e.g., environmental regimes) or in different issue domains (e.g., environmental regimes and economic regimes). The general expectation in this regard is that synergy will be more common in cases of interactions occurring in the same issue domain, whereas interference will be a more frequent occurrence in cross-domain interactions. So, for example, the ozone/climate interaction is positive, whereas many fear that interactions between environmental regimes and the trade regime are likely to be negative. The logic of this expectation is understandable; regimes operating in separate issue domains are more likely to be based on fundamentally different principles than regimes operating in the same issue domain. Yet there is no reason simply to accept this proposition as an unalterable fact of life. To take a prominent example, there are ways to alleviate—if not to eliminate—tensions between the trade regime and various environmental regimes operating at the international level.

Intended vs. Unintended Interactions

This discussion leads to another distinction that is important in efforts to understand the landscape of institutional interplay. Interplay between distinct regimes can and often does take the form of un-intended interactions. This is true especially in settings where the density of governance systems is great and growing while respon-sibility for creating and implementing individual regimes falls to different legislative committees and administrative agencies. In the United States, for example, the National Oceanic and Atmospheric Administration (NOAA) is responsible for administering the regime governing commercial fishing; the Department of the Interior has the lead with regard to the administration of the regime governing offshore oil and gas development. Although the resultant inter-actions generally are unintended, the occurrence of interference between the two systems is common. Much the same concern arises at the international level, where there are tensions between arrange-ments dealing with trade and biosafety and between the trade regime and efforts to protect threatened species, like various types of tunas and turtles.

As these examples suggest, however, unintended interactions can and often do give way to intentional efforts to pursue different goals through deliberate actions involving institutional interplay.[6] To start on a positive note, it is not surprising that those who are frustrated by the difficulties of making progress under the Kyoto Protocol regard actions under the Montreal Protocol aimed at re-ducing emissions of greenhouse gases as an attractive prospect. For some, the idea of buying time through this process to enhance the effectiveness of the climate regime has become a matter of intense concern.[7] But intentional efforts to take advantage of institutional interplay often take the form of initiatives designed to promote the agendas of specific actors in the relevant settings. The debates about whether to address issues of biosafety under the provisions of the trade regime or the 2000 Cartagena Protocol on Biosafety to the Convention on Biological Diversity and whether to deal with off-shore oil and gas development under the provisions of the outer continental shelf lands regime or broader arrangements relating to ocean governance offer dramatic examples of such interest-driven interactions.[8] The next section turns to the theme of the politics of interplay in a systematic fashion.

Forms of Interplay

Meanwhile, it is worth taking note of several distinctions about forms of interactions that will help to make sense of the landscape of institutional interplay.[9] The usual starting point is to think about cases of overlap, in which two regimes that have little or nothing to do with one another in substantive terms generate actions that affect the success of one or both of the regimes in question.[10] The trade-environment interactions are illustrative in these terms. For the most part those concerned with trade and with hazardous wastes or endangered species of fauna and flora have little to do with one another. They operate in different agencies within national governments and interact with others in international venues that are largely issue specific. Nevertheless, it turns out that the governance systems they produce interact with one another in practice. The usual procedure then is to look for ways to ease tensions after the fact or to exploit de facto opportunities for synergy in the sense of looking for adjustments designed to facilitate positive relations between the relevant regimes.

There are other forms of institutional interplay that are worth bearing in mind as well. Regimes addressing specific issues are almost always embedded in the deep structures of the socioeconomic and political systems in which they operate. For example, the regimes dealing with international trade, climate change, and ozone depletion all assume that they will operate in a system of sovereign states in which there is no supranational government in the ordinary sense of the term.[11] The regimes dealing with a host of marine issues in the United States all assume that they will operate under a common system featuring federalism in intergovernmental relations and a separation of authority among a number of agencies at the national level. These are significant common bonds. They do not preclude conflicts such as those arising between the regimes for commercial fishing and offshore oil and gas development in the United States, but they do place important boundaries on the scope and intensity of interplay among regimes dealing with specific issues.

Beyond this lie cases involving multiple regimes that are nested into a common framework and clustered regimes that make up what are known as regime complexes. One way to manage interplay is to create an organic act or framework convention that provides a common basis for regimes dealing with a collection of related activities. In the United States, for example, there are organic acts for the Park Service, the Forest Service, and the Bureau of Land Management, which is responsible for the residual public domain. The UN Convention on the Law of the Sea (UNCLOS) plays a similar role at the international level. In each case the idea is to create a common foundation for regimes dealing with specific activities, such as fishing, shipping, oil and gas development, waste disposal, and so forth. A related but distinct situation arises in cases where there is no organic act or framework convention, yet issue-specific regimes nevertheless form a cluster of interactive but non-hierarchical arrangements operating in the same issue domain.[12] The distinct arrangements that make up the Antarctic Treaty System at the international level or the management of migratory species at the domestic level illustrate what are now treated in the scientific literature as regime complexes. A critical step in thinking about issues of institutional interplay, therefore, is to locate a given case within the overarching landscape of interplay and then consider possible trajectories along which interactions between or among the regimes in question may progress.

The Politics of Interplay

Institutional interplay is political all the way down. We must expect that actors operating in settings involving actual or potential interactions between or among regimes dealing with specific issues will pursue their own interests energetically. There are those—especially in the scientific community—who are concerned about the performance of governance systems in holistic terms. But far more common are actors whose efforts focus on advancing the interests of energy companies, fishers, tourism companies, defenders of the integrity of ecosystems, citizens exposed to threats to human health, and so forth. These actors will look at institutional interplay from the perspective of promoting their own causes, thus embracing links that seem beneficial from their perspective and opposing links that seem problematic in these terms. Broadly speaking, we can separate the politics of interplay into two main categories, one centering on the establishment of new regimes or the reform of existing regimes and the other featuring the administration of regimes once they are in place.[13] These categories overlap to some degree. Those responsible for implementing a given regime, for instance, may become advocates for institutional reforms they believe would make the regime more successful in fulfilling its goals. Still, it makes sense to divide the politics of interplay into the domains of regime (re)formation and administration.

Regime Formation

A number of concerns relating to institutional interplay can arise in processes of regime formation. In some cases the parties are motivated to contribute to the development of a regime complex, thus creating new regimes that fit into a complex but that are not regarded as suitable for treatment as amendments to an existing arrangement. In the case of the Antarctic Treaty System, for instance, new elements covering such matters as commercial fishing have been articulated in the form of separate treaties (e.g., the Convention on the Conservation of Antarctic Marine Living Resources) in order to accommodate provisions that would not fit comfortably into the original Antarctic Treaty and also to allow for a somewhat different membership. An intriguing development in this arena centered on the tension arising during the 1980s between those who advocated the creation of a distinct regime covering mining and those pushing for the addition of a protocol to the original Antarctic Treaty that would, among other things, ban mining activities.[14] Mining advocates were able to gain agreement on the terms of a new regime articulated in the 1988 Convention on the Regulation of Antarctic Mineral Resource Activities, but this exercise in institutional interplay collapsed abruptly when key parties defected from the coalition supporting the convention. As a result, the effort to create a distinct regime covering mineral resource activities failed and was succeeded in short order by the adoption in 1991 of a protocol to the original Antarctic Treaty on environmental protection. The upshot was a decision, preferred by those interested mainly in environmental protection, to add elements to the original Antarctic Treaty rather than an action, preferred by commercial interests, that would have increased institutional interplay by adopting a separate treaty, thereby adding a new component to the Antarctic Treaty System.

In other cases the focus on interplay features an effort to create a new institutional foundation that will serve to promote integration and enhance coherence in an issue domain characterized by the existence of a number of arrangements covering specific activities. In the United States the development of organic acts designed to provide platforms for an array of more specific arrangements pertaining to the national parks, the national forests, or the residual public domain exemplifies this type of institutional interplay.[15] The Federal Land Policy and Management Act of 1976, for instance, provides an institutional foundation for the Bureau of Land Management's efforts to address a variety of activities—from grazing to mining and on to recreation—taking place on federal lands not included in separate systems like the national parks, forests, fish and wildlife refuges, and so forth. The current effort to reach agreement on the terms of legislation known as Oceans 21 is motivated by the argument that existing regimes dealing with marine issues constitute a hodgepodge leading to both gaps and overlaps that makes it impossible to govern human activities in coastal waters in a coherent fashion.[16] At the international level the negotiations that eventuated in adopting the 1982 UN Convention on the Law of the Sea reflect a similar concern. This convention is built on consensus regarding the proposition that interplay among a range of distinct regimes covering shipping, fishing, mining, environmental protection, and so forth would lead to institutional fragmentation in the absence of a foundational arrangement designed to promote coherence in this realm.[17]

In some cases, by contrast, regimes are created, at least in part, to provide an institutional base for those desiring to pursue interests likely to be subordinated in the absence of independent support. One rationale for developing the 2000 Cartagena Protocol on Biosafety, for instance, was to provide institutional support for those desiring to impose restrictions or even prohibitions on the dissemination of genetically modified organisms (GMOs) and believing that their concern would be marginalized if the regulation of such organisms was left entirely to the World Trade Organization (WTO).[18] A similar concern in the United States motivates those who see the introduction of procedures calling for coastal and marine spatial planning (CMSP) as an institutional mechanism to regulate activities like offshore oil and gas development and commercial fishing in areas that are fragile in biophysical terms or not understood well enough to allow actors to make informed decisions about their activities.[19] Whereas the discussion in the preceding paragraph centered on actions intended to avoid or mitigate the dangers of fragmentation, the issue here involves strategic uses of interplay in order to promote or defend the interests of specific players in the system who recognize that the rights and rules of applicable governance systems can play an important role in guiding the course of human-environment relations.

Institutional Administration

Consider now uses of institutional interplay on the part of those responsible for implementing or administering existing regimes. One prominent strategy features using other regimes to lend support to those seeking to enhance the effectiveness of specific regimes. The role of the ozone regime in reducing emissions of greenhouse gases, referred to in the preceding section, is a prominent example. It makes perfect sense for those endeavoring to make a success of the climate regime to reach out to the ozone regime for support, even though the ozone regime is a distinct arrangement with no formal link to the climate regime. Conversely, those who oppose key provisions or even the existence of a particular regime are sometimes able to use the provisions of another regime to promote their cause. At the international level those opposed to environmental regimes often claim that the trade regime's provisions trump key provisions of arrangements like those of the climate and biological diversity regimes. Similar combative uses of institutional interplay are common at the national level as well. A prominent example centers on the use of the regime dealing with outer continental shelf lands to justify oil and gas development in areas that seem suitable for conservation measures under the terms of the regime dealing with commercial fisheries or even preservation measures under the terms of the regime dealing with marine sanctuaries.[20]

Beyond these strategic uses of interplay between or among existing regimes lies a set of issues of a more conventional administrative nature. Some of these issues involve efforts to negotiate a modus vivendi between regimes that overlap but lack any explicit provisions regarding the treatment of such overlaps. Prominent examples deal with sorting out relations between the international regime covering trade and environmental regimes containing provisions relating to trade, such as the ozone regime, the regime dealing with trade in endangered species, and the regime covering transboundary movements of hazardous wastes. Some observers anticipate open clashes in such cases; they often assume that the political strength of the trade regime will make it victorious in such encounters. But by and large this has not occurred, as those responsible for administering the regimes in question have exhibited a preference for dealing with such issues on an ad hoc and low-key basis.[21] A related question arises in cases in which there is a need to settle disputes involving institutional interplay. Predictably, supporters of the trade regime argue that disputes involving environment-trade interactions should be handled through the efforts of WTO dispute settlement panels; not surprisingly, those associated with the relevant environmental regimes resist this approach. This is a contentious issue that does not lend itself to a general solution; it is likely to be handled on an ad hoc or case-by-case basis in the foreseeable future.

Institutional Reform?

The politics of institutional interplay focus for the most part on concrete issues. Should the coastal plain of the Arctic National

Wildlife Refuge in the United States be designated as wilderness? Should standards relating to GMOs be developed under the WTO or the Cartagena Protocol? Does the prohibition on transboundary movements of hazardous wastes constitute a violation of WTO rules? Under the circumstances it is easy to understand why many informed observers fear increasing fragmentation in the realm of environmental governance, a trend that could cripple efforts to enhance social welfare regarding an issue that is growing in importance at all levels of social organization. This is a worry that motivates many proposals aimed at reducing fragmentation and enhancing integration both at the international level (e.g., proposals to turn the UN Environment Programme into a World Environment Organization) and at the national level (e.g., the proposal in the United States to create a new governance system for ocean spaces featuring the principles and practices of coastal and marine spatial planning).[22] Yet such restructuring is easier said than done. Given the multiplicity of stakeholders involved, the intensity of their interests, and the existence of numerous veto players, finding ways to make progress is a daunting challenge.[23] This is especially true at the international level, where there is no government in the ordinary sense of the term and the pressure to strive for maximum winning coalitions is great. But such problems are also common in the US political system and others like it, in which divided governments are unable to put together winning coalitions that include majorities in both houses of bicameral legislatures along with the support of the chief executive.

Managing Institutional Interplay

As the density of governance systems operating in a political space grows, it is to be expected that the challenge of managing interactions between or among them in order to maximize positive outcomes and minimize the negative effects of clashes will emerge as an increasingly prominent concern. There is a long history of efforts to address this issue in domestic settings, though interplay management focusing on environmental regimes is a relatively new concern. At the international level, where there is less experience with complex governance systems, the issue is not so familiar. But with the establishment of hundreds of multilateral environmental agreements—not to mention the growth of well-developed governance systems in other issue domains, including those dealing with trade and monetary concerns—interplay management is emerging rapidly as a priority theme. What can we say about the strategies available for managing interplay in this context? Here I identify and discuss four families of strategies featuring (i) adjudication, (ii) negotiated settlements, (iii) place-based management, and (iv) the emergence of regime complexes.

Adjudication

The hallmark of adjudication is reliance on a court or some other trusted third party mechanism (e.g., an arbitral tribunal) to make authoritative decisions about issues arising from institutional interplay. This is a common practice in many domestic settings, where courts are regularly called upon to make decisions about the application or reach of distinct environmental regimes. It is less common at other levels, where the use of courts to adjudicate competing claims is uncommon. Even so, there is some experience with the use of adjudication at other levels. The manor courts in medieval England, for example, appear to have played a significant role in resolving disputes regarding various aspects of commonfield agricultural practices.[24] Although the use of courts to address such matters is not common at the international level, there is relevant experience here too, such as the arbitration regarding pollution caused by the Trail Smelter crossing the border between Canada and the United States and the International Court of Justice's decision relating to the limits of Canadian and US jurisdiction over the area known as Georges Bank.[25] For the most part courts and other third parties have little capacity to address substantive issues relating to environmental governance. Consequently, they normally approach issues involving institutional interplay through a search for clues in the relevant documents or by applying standards relating to proximity in time or degree of specificity of the applicable legal instruments.[26] The results may have the virtue of authoritativeness, so that differences between the parties are resolved once and for all. But there is little reason to expect that they will yield environmental regimes that are well matched to the principal features of the socioecological settings in which they operate.

Negotiated Settlement

An alternative strategy highlights the role of negotiated settlements. This approach does not call for authoritative decisions of the sort emerging from the rulings of courts or arbitral tribunals; instead, the goal is to come up with some practical measures that the relevant actors are prepared to live with on a day-to-day basis. The use of this strategy is most likely in settings where those responsible for administering regimes are searching for pragmatic solutions to concrete problems; it seldom plays a role in the processes leading to the creation of regimes in the first place. A pragmatic approach of this sort is familiar in domestic settings in which agencies charged with the administration of distinct regimes (e.g., the regimes dealing with land use on the one hand and clean air and water on the other) search for amicable ways to alleviate tensions arising from their activities.[27] Similar efforts are now emerging at the international level in order to arrive at workable approaches to alleviating tensions between the international trade regime and a variety of environmental regimes that include trade-related provisions. Although the outcomes are likely to lack the authoritativeness that distinguishes adjudication or other third-party procedures, this strategy can produce accommodation at the level of day-to-day interactions without raising issues of principle that would be difficult or impossible to resolve in more general terms.

Place-Based Management

A third family of strategies relevant to interplay management includes procedures that center on what has become known as place-based management. The essential idea here is to focus on spatially and (often) functionally defined areas and apply some form of zoning or spatial planning so as to determine where the provisions of different regimes will apply. A prominent case in point involves the management of the Great Barrier Reef in Australia.[28] Here, the zones range from areas in which multiple use is the prevailing order to areas that are off-limits to almost all human activities. No effort is made under this procedure to arrive at conclusions of a general nature regarding interactions between distinct regimes; rather, the idea is to maximize the fit between governance systems and socioecological conditions by bringing to bear a suite of procedures often referred to collectively as spatial planning.[29] The premise underlying this approach is that resolving tensions arising from institutional interactions in some general sense is not necessary; the pragmatic way forward is to work out such matters in specific situations in such a way as to avoid or mitigate the problems of fragmentation or incoherence that arise when multiple regimes operate in the same spatial domain without coordination. Of course, the success of this approach depends on both devising procedures to delimit suitable spaces and garnering the support of key stakeholders who have legitimate interests in what goes on in these spaces. But preliminary results dealing with coastal and marine spatial planning in a number of countries are promising.

Regime Complexes

A fourth approach encompasses strategies that turn the third strategy around and direct attention to what those interested in international governance call regime complexes.[30] The critical step here is to focus on functionally and (sometimes) spatially defined areas and develop interrelated collections of regime elements that fall somewhere along a continuum ranging from fully integrated to fully decentralized arrangements. This has led to analyses dealing with collections of arrangements addressing plant genetic resources, climate, threatened or endangered species, marine pollution, and so forth. Experience suggests that there are cases in which there is room for assembling sets of regime elements that are not hierarchically integrated but work well together even when it is not feasible politically to reach agreement on the provisions of a fully integrated governance system. Once such a complex is established and recognized, it may be feasible politically to strengthen the resultant governance system over time by tightening the links between the elements of the complex and adding new elements that serve to enhance the coverage of the governance system. Although this approach does not offer an effective means of dealing with the management issues arising in all cases of institutional interplay, it does seem promising in situations in which tensions are rising but the politics of the situation make expectations of a fully integrated governance system unrealistic.

Conclusion

The need to come to terms with issues of complex environmental governance is a fact of life at all levels of social organization. Institutional overlaps sometimes arise as unintended consequences of efforts to create regimes dealing with individual environmental problems or with problems arising in other issue domains. However, it does not take long for major stakeholders and other interested parties to recognize the emergence of interactions and begin to think about ways not only to protect their own interests in such situations but also to use such interactions to advance their own causes. This poses an additional challenge to those interested in interplay management. A number of families of strategies have emerged from efforts to address this challenge. Although none of them constitutes a panacea in the sense of a straightforward method of resolving tensions among distinct governance systems, there is no reason to reach pessimistic conclusions about the broader consequences arising from the operation of these systems. The evidence that has accumulated so far makes it clear that institutional interactions can produce positive or even synergistic results under some circumstances and that various approaches to interplay management can prove effective at least on a case-by-case basis.[31]

CHAPTER FIVE
VERTICAL INTERPLAY

MASTERING MULTILEVEL GOVERNANCE

Environmental problems regularly cut across levels defined in biophysical and socioeconomic terms. Although some problems (e.g., harvesting a local stock of fish sustainably, cleaning up a spatially limited toxic waste site) are local in scope, others involve much broader domains. Climate change, to take a prominent example, is a multilevel concern. Human actions anywhere on the planet (e.g., burning coal in a specific power plant, using gasoline in an individual automobile, cutting trees in a particular forest) can add to concentrations of greenhouse gases in the atmosphere and, therefore, contribute to climate change on a planetary scale. Climate change, in turn, affects the well-being of people everywhere, though the nature and severity of the impacts will depend on a range of biophysical and socioeconomic factors. It is possible that some may benefit, at least in the early stages, from the impacts of climate change. But no one will be unaffected, especially as its pace accelerates in the coming decades. Much the same is true regarding other large-scale biophysical changes. Sea-level rise is a matter of utmost concern to those residing in a host of low-lying island states; desertification is a major threat to those engaged in dryland agriculture in many places; melting glaciers pose a severe challenge to those whose livelihoods are tied to rivers that currently flow freely throughout the year.

Similar observations are in order about interactions among governance systems operating at different levels of social organization.[1] Global problems like climate change call for global responses in the form of what are known as multilateral environmental agreements (e.g., the UN Framework Convention on Climate Change). But for the most part responsibility for implementing commitments made in such agreements rests with the governments of the individual member states. Member states, in turn, vary substantially with regard to how such responsibilities are handled. Some are highly centralized, so that the authority to take the initiative regarding matters of environmental governance lies more or less exclusively with the national government. But many others are more decentralized, a feature that makes it necessary for national governments to engage with local and regional governments about fulfilling commitments embedded in international agreements as well as opens up opportunities for governments operating at different levels of social organization to take the initiative in coming to terms with issues of environmental governance. It is important to bear in mind as well that these vertical interactions can and often do play out in combination with the sorts of horizontal interplay discussed in the preceding chapter. Although some players are wrestling with interactions between the trade regime and various environmental regimes at the international level, for example, others are likely to be engaged in more or less complex interactions about the same issues across two or more levels of social organization in domestic settings.

This chapter focuses on issues of multilevel governance that affect the treatment of environmental problems. Once again, the analysis proceeds in three steps. The first section deals with multilevel patterns of public authority that have significant implications for the treatment of environmental issues; it draws attention to differences in authority structures and what they mean for those endeavoring to solve environmental problems. The next section turns to the subject of multilevel environmental politics. The point of departure here is the observation that self-interested actors will endeavor to take advantage of various features of multilevel governance to advance their own causes in addressing environmental issues. The third substantive section then turns to the theme of multilevel environmental management. Just as chapter 4 examined strategies for managing horizontal interplay, the issue of strategies designed to address questions of multilevel management comes into focus here. The fundamental challenge throughout is to find ways to take advantage of systems of multilevel governance in efforts to solve environmental problems and, at the same time, minimize cross-level complications that can impede efforts to make progress in this realm.

Multilevel Public Authority

Public authority in the sense of legitimate power to make decisions on behalf of a society regarding matters of common concern is socially constructed. We can ask whether the actual pattern of authority in a given society conforms to the pattern articulated in its constitution or constitutive documents, and we can examine patterns of authority as they evolve over time in any given society. But the allocation of authority across levels of social organization varies greatly from one society to another, developing in a distinctive manner within individual societies. These differences can be expected to have significant consequences for handling matters of environmental governance.

As a point of departure consider a spectrum ranging from extreme centralization regarding the allocation of authority to extreme decentralization in this realm.[2] Some countries (e.g., France, China) have political systems in which public authority is highly centralized so that local and even regional governments have little or no authority to make decisions about environmental matters on their own. On paper, at least, municipal governments in these countries must seek authorization from the center if and when they want to address questions like the treatment of air and water pollution affecting the well-being of their citizens. At the opposite extreme are political systems that are so decentralized that the center has little or no authority to make decisions on behalf of society as a whole. The US government operating under the Articles of

Confederation during the 1770s and 1780s, for example, had little authority to make decisions about matters of common concern (e.g., raising an army, imposing taxes) without the consent of the individual states.[3] A contemporary example that is similar in character is the European Union. Although the European Parliament and the Council of the European Union have slowly acquired limited authority in some areas, collective action on the part of the union in most areas requires the explicit or at least implicit consent of the member states.[4]

Most political systems lie somewhere along this (de)centralization spectrum with regard to the allocation of authority to address matters of environmental governance. Consider Canada, a confederal system, and the United States, a federal system, in these terms. Under the terms of the Constitution of 1982, the national government of Canada must seek the consent of the governments of the individual provinces in order to assume obligations (e.g., commitments regarding emissions of greenhouse gases) that will bind the society as a whole.[5] The US Constitution does grant authority to the federal government regarding a variety of specific issues, including the handling of foreign relations, national security, and the regulation of interstate commerce. But under the Tenth Amendment to the Constitution the individual states retain authority over all matters not explicitly awarded to the federal government.[6] Because most environmental issues were local or regional concerns during the last quarter of the eighteenth century, the Constitution does not speak directly to the role of the federal government in the realm of environmental governance.

The Federal Role

Yet today the federal government is deeply involved in a wide variety of environmental issues, ranging from managing commercial fisheries in coastal waters to protecting endangered species and on to regulating toxic wastes and air and water pollution. How has this transformation regarding the allocation of authority come about? For one thing the federal government has turned to general provisions of the Constitution and applied them to address environmental issues. Because the federal government has exclusive authority over matters involving foreign relations, for instance, it is able to deal with matters like migratory species, transboundary air pollution, or climate change that require the negotiation of international agreements in the form of conventions, treaties, and executive agreements. The federal government also has the authority to manage the public domain—land and associated natural resources belonging to the nation as a whole. With the Louisiana Purchase in 1803 and the annexation or conquest of the west in the ensuing decades, this source of authority loomed larger and larger. But beyond this the federal government has sought to devise novel interpretations of the provisions of the Constitution as a means of expanding its authority over environmental matters.[7] The Commerce Clause of the Constitution, for example, has provided a basis for asserting authority over issues relating to air and water pollution. The authority of the federal government regarding interstate compacts has come into play in cases like creating a regime to manage the waters of the Colorado River. The idea of the public trust has been broadened from its origins as a basis for state authority to become a source of federal authority over major rivers, lakes, and, more recently, coastal waters now extending out to the outer limits of the Exclusive Economic Zone.

State and Local Governments

Although these actions have produced a dramatic increase in the federal government's authority, state and local governments have not disappeared from the scene when it comes to matters of environmental governance. Zoning is largely a local affair. State governments assert authority over developments involving lands belonging to them, their coastal zones, and state waters that extend to a distance of three miles from the coast. In some cases states refuse to recognize the authority of the federal government over specific matters (e.g., requirements set forth in some of the provisions of the Clean Air Act Amendments of 1990) and adopt the position that they will refuse to implement federal decisions regarding such matters within their jurisdictions. More recently states have begun to take actions regarding environmental issues as a result of growing frustration with the federal government's inability or unwillingness to act. Climate change is a prominent example.[8] California has acted on its own to address the problem of greenhouse gas emissions, enacting the 2006 Global Warming Solutions Act (often known as AB 32) and working toward the promulgation of regulations needed to move the provisions of this act from paper to practice. Groups of states have banded together to take action regarding climate change through the Western Climate Initiative and the Regional Greenhouse Gas Initiative in the northeast. Some states have sought to move forward by seeking exemptions under the provisions of the federal Clean Air Act Amendments of 1990, allowing them to raise fuel economy standards, filing lawsuits requiring the federal government to recognize greenhouse gases as pollutants under the terms of the Clean Air Act, and asserting that the nuisance doctrine gives them authority to act regarding greenhouse gas emissions in the absence of federal action in this realm. Some states have even entered into agreements with counterparts in other countries as a means of making progress with regard to environmental issues. California, acting again as a leader regarding environmental matters, has entered into an agreement with Jiangsu Province in China to cooperate on environmental matters and is negotiating with the State of Acre in Brazil about ways to cooperate in fulfilling the provisions of the Global Warming Solutions Act and devising arrangements designed to slow the pace of deforestation.[9]

A Complex Mosaic

The result is a complex and shifting mosaic of governance systems applicable to environmental matters involving arrangements operating at different levels of social organization. In the case of coasts and oceans, for example, local governments assert authority over public beaches, state governments have assumed authority over development in the coastal zone, state governments exercise authority in state waters extending from the coast to a limit of three miles offshore, the federal government has authority beyond state waters extending to the outer limit of the Exclusive Economic

Zone (EEZ) located two hundred nautical miles from the coast, and international management under the terms of the UN Convention on the Law of the Sea (UNCLOS) takes over beyond the limits of the EEZ.

However, many environmental issues do not divide neatly into these jurisdictional compartments. Consider wildlife management as an illustrative case. In the United States the authority to manage wildlife has generally resided with state governments, even in the case of federal lands located within the jurisdiction of states.[10] But the federal government retains the authority to manage wildlife located on federal lands in cases in which it determines that state laws are incompatible with federal laws, and the federal government has asserted authority under the Commerce Clause to regulate trade in wildlife products (e.g., exotic feathers, walrus ivory) crossing state boundaries. Where highly migratory species are involved (e.g., caribou, various species of birds), management requires negotiating international agreements with other range states. The United States and Canada, for example, have entered into agreements regarding the management of caribou crossing the national boundary between Alaska and Yukon Territory, and there are numerous bilateral and multilateral agreements dealing with migratory birds.[11] Whereas local governments constitute the first line of attack when it comes to tackling the problem of air pollution, the federal government soon gets into the act when airborne pollutants cross state boundaries, and international agreements are needed when the pollution crosses national boundaries (e.g., sulfur dioxide and nitrogen oxide crossing the boundary between the United States and Canada in eastern North America). There are even cases in which local regulations designed to reduce pollution in the immediate vicinity of a source can give rise to interstate problems by mandating measures (e.g., taller smokestacks) that increase the volume of pollutants traveling across state boundaries and becoming matters of federal concern in the process.

All these multilevel relationships are dynamic; they are subject to change over time not only in formal terms but also in more informal terms reflected in shifting content of relevant practices. The expansion of federal jurisdiction over environmental issues in the United States constitutes a dramatic example. Equally interesting are the recent efforts of state and even local governments to assert authority to address pressing concerns on which the federal government is unable or unwilling to act. Developments regarding climate change provide a striking illustration of this development. Not only are cities and states taking the initiative in regulating greenhouse gas emissions; they are also entering into agreements with their counterparts in other countries to make common cause in addressing the problem of climate change.[12] Over twelve hundred cities, towns, and counties, for example, now belong to Local Governments for Sustainability (also known as ICLEI), an organization dedicated to taking the initiative regarding reductions in emissions of greenhouse gases on a worldwide basis. Individual cities have assumed a leading role in taking steps needed to enhance their capacity to adapt to the consequences of climate change once they begin to take effect.

Supranational Authority

In this age of large-scale (often global) challenges of environmental governance, it is important to think clearly about patterns of public authority beyond the nation state. International society is a case of extreme decentralization with regard to the allocation of public authority. As Article 2(7) of the United Nations Charter puts it, "Nothing contained in the present Charter shall authorize the United Nations to intervene in matters which are essentially within the domestic jurisdiction of any state."[13] Yet limited exceptions to this feature of the deep structure of international society relevant to environmental governance have begun to emerge. The Meeting of the Parties to the Montreal Protocol on ozone-depleting substances (which is now virtually universal), for example, has the authority to make decisions about matters such as the acceleration of phase-out schedules for specific chemicals that are binding on the members without any requirement for ratification on the part of individual member states. The anarchic character of international society also constitutes a motivating force for those who have begun to think of global civil society as a source of governance initiatives and to explore the prospects for launching various forms of private governance (e.g., the Forest Stewardship Council).[14] But the fact remains that international society constitutes an example of a highly decentralized political system with regard to allocating public authority. Most decisions at this level of social organization regarding initiatives designed to address large-scale environmental concerns require the consent of the member states to enter into force. Individual members must assume responsibility as well for implementing the terms of international environmental agreements within their own jurisdictions in the absence of a supranational government capable of bringing pressure to bear on them to live up to the terms of the obligations articulated in these agreements.

Multilevel Environmental Politics

In a world of self-interested actors seeking to advance their own causes whenever and however possible, it will come as no surprise that individual players at every level of social organization approach multilevel governance in political terms. They may see vertical interplay as an opportunity to make progress on environmental issues by shifting from one level to another when they find themselves blocked at another level. Conversely, they may look to multilevel governance for opportunities to block the adoption or the implementation of measures they oppose for one reason or another. There is every reason to expect that the vertical interactions that give rise to multilevel governance will become battlegrounds for all parties concerned when it comes to moving forward or defending the status quo regarding matters of environmental governance.

International Initiatives

The role of multilevel governance is particularly important whenever international efforts are required due to the fact that international society lacks a government in the ordinary sense of the term. Coordination between international initiatives and national actions is required in order to make progress regarding all large-scale environmental issues. In cases like climate change and the loss of biological diversity, for instance, international agreements do not become legally binding on individual signatories until national governments ratify them, and they do not enter into force until enough of the signatories have ratified them to fulfill the requirements articulated in the agreements themselves. For many countries ratification makes little difference unless and until the obligations assumed in an international agreement are incorporated into the provisions of implementing legislation within individual member states and responsibility for implementation is assigned to specific agencies at the national level. In the United States, for example, Title IV of the Clean Air Act Amendments of 1990 authorizes the implementation of the 1987 Montreal Protocol on Substances that Deplete the Ozone Layer within the United States and assigns responsibility for carrying out the terms of this legislation to the Environmental Protection Agency. At the operational level the EPA relies on its regional offices around the country and on state-level environmental protection agencies within individual states to oversee the actions required to ensure compliance with the terms of the protocol.

This opens up a range of opportunities for those opposed to or skeptical about innovations in environmental governance to block or slow down the development of new arrangements. Opponents can start by taking steps to prevent the ratification of international agreements. A handful of senators in the United States, for example, have managed to block the ratification of the 1982 UN Convention on the Law of the Sea despite the fact that both Republican and Democratic administrations as well as a majority of members of the Senate Committee on Foreign Relations have consistently advocated ratification. And the prospects for passing domestic legislation regarding ocean governance, inspired in part by the need to implement various elements of UNCLOS, are not encouraging at this stage. Nor is this an isolated case to be accounted for in terms of idiosyncratic factors. Although the United States has been a leader in creating and strengthening the ozone regime, it has failed to ratify a host of multilateral environmental agreements negotiated more recently, including the Convention on Biological Diversity, the Kyoto Protocol to the climate convention, and the Stockholm Convention on Persistent Organic Pollutants.

Just as multilevel environmental politics can slow or block the development of international governance systems, domestic pressures can become driving forces that lead to progress at the international level. A striking example involves the development of the 1991 bilateral Air Quality Agreement between Canada and the United States.[15] The problem of acid rain associated with sulfur dioxide and nitrogen oxide emissions originating in the United States and flowing into Canada had festered throughout the 1980s with little sign of progress at the international level. But the passage of the Clean Air Act Amendments of 1990 mandating radical reductions in emissions of these pollutants at the national level broke the logjam at the international level. The successful conclusion of the 1991 bilateral agreement followed in short order once the internal political battle over this issue was resolved in the United States. Similarly, subnational governments, including cities as well as states, have become active in the effort to bring pressure to bear on national governments to fulfill the promise of the 2007 Bali Roadmap calling for the strengthening of the Kyoto Protocol and/or the negotiation of a new and more comprehensive international agreement on climate change. So far these efforts have not borne fruit in terms of their primary objective. The meeting of the Conference of the Parties in Copenhagen in 2009 (COP 15) produced only a policy document known as the Copenhagen Accord; no new legally binding agreement on climate change is in sight at this time.[16] Nevertheless, this process has activated a variety of subnational governments and nonstate actors to play increasingly active and influential roles in the realm of multilevel environmental governance. We have moved into an era when subnational actors are no longer content to leave the treatment of large-scale environmental issues exclusively in the hands of national governments. The more complex system of interactions resulting from this development in the realm of environmental politics is here to stay.

States as Environmental Leaders

Nor is multilevel environmental politics limited to situations in which the negotiation or implementation of international agreements is at stake. Similar patterns of advocacy and opposition are evident with regard to national environmental politics.[17] In the United States California has long been a leader in efforts to tackle environmental issues aggressively. At least since the 1970s the state has been a force for progressive action relating to issues like the treatment of air pollution, the establishment of fuel efficiency standards for automobiles, the management of the coastal zone, and, more recently, the response to climate change. Because California is so large (well over 10 percent of Americans live in the state), the state's actions regarding environmental issues have affected environmental politics at the national level, either by influencing the strategies of corporations or by setting the pace with regard to developing federal legislation. But California is not alone in this domain. A coalition of states led by Massachusetts won a decision in the US Supreme Court affirming that greenhouse gases are pollutants under the terms of the Clean Air Act Amendments of 1990.[18] And other states have sought to apply the nuisance doctrine as a basis for state-level actions relating to emissions of greenhouse gases in the absence of federal action to address this increasingly important problem.[19]

Opposition Forces

Conversely, those wishing to stop or delay action regarding environmental issues also resort to multilevel environmental politics in efforts to promote their causes. The American federal system allows for—even encourages—recurrent battles regarding allocating authority between the federal government and state governments over matters of environmental governance. Because federal measures often rely on implementation through state-level agencies, states can dig in their heels and refuse to act regarding policies they dislike. For example, a number of states have refused to apply federal standards designed to reduce emissions of pollutants from new power plants or to acknowledge that large-scale renovations of existing power plants should be subjected to new source-review standards.[20] Even local governments can balk at the implementation of actions in the form of mandates coming down from above. In California, for instance, municipal and county governments sometimes resist state regulations designed to protect coastal assets under the provisions of the state's coastal act. The outcomes of such battles are difficult to predict; numerous factors come into play in specific cases. But the importance of multilevel environmental politics as a force influencing the course of human-environment relations is undeniable.

Multilevel Environmental Management

As the preceding discussion makes clear, multilevel politics is not only a prominent feature of the landscape of environmental governance; it can also emerge as a force leading either to synergy or to gridlock under the conditions prevailing in specific cases. Just as the final section of chapter 4 focused on managing horizontal interplay, this section directs attention to managing multilevel environmental governance in such a way as to enhance individual well-being and improve social welfare. What constitutes progress in this realm may be subject to disagreement from those adhering to different value systems and espousing different philosophies regarding state-society relations. Nevertheless, the avoidance of gridlock arising from the dynamics of multilevel governance is a matter of common concern. In this section I discuss four families of strategies that are available to those concerned with this challenge: (i) adopting the principle of subsidiarity, (ii) creating cross-level steering mechanisms, (iii) using adjudication to resolve differences, and (iv) resolving such issues through the adoption of legislation or, in extreme cases, constitutional amendments.

Subsidiarity

The principle of subsidiarty asserts that environmental issues should be dealt with at the lowest level of political organization in a position to address the issues effectively.[21] Local governments should be responsible for systems of zoning designed to minimize conflicts among neighbors relating to environmental issues (e.g., the generation of pollutants that are harmful to the owners of adjacent properties). Regional or state governments should take responsibility for setting standards regarding the use of wetlands located in their coastal zones. In the final analysis international mechanisms will be necessary to solve problems like long-range transboundary air pollution or the emission of greenhouse gases. The appeal of this principle is easy to understand; the idea is to locate authority and responsibility with decision-makers who are close to the relevant problems and best informed about the nature of these problems and their impacts on affected parties. But the applicability of this strategy is severely limited. As I observed in the introduction to this chapter, large-scale problems like climate change affect the well-being of those residing in specific communities. Equally important, local arrangements, like building codes and public transport systems, have direct implications for the evolution of global problems like climate change. This does not mean that the principle of subsidiarity is irrelevant and should be discarded in a world in which multilevel governance has become a prominent consideration; there are some problems that local and regional governments can and should handle. But the idea of subsidiarity is not a panacea under contemporary conditions; multilevel problems will require multilevel solutions.

Cross-Level Steering Mechanisms

A second approach features the creation of regimes designed to facilitate collaboration across levels of social organization. There is actually a long history of cross-level arrangements in areas like the management of fish and wildlife where state departments of fish and game in the US system have developed effective working relationships with the relevant agencies in the US Department of the Interior and the National Oceanic and Atmospheric Administration. Recently, the idea of cross-level collaboration has become popular in the form of what is generally called comanagement.[22] The essential feature of comanagement is the development of bodies that allow for and even encourage collaborative decision making among those who use natural resources, typically operating at a local or spatially restricted level, and policy-makers, who are located at the state or even the federal level. The users not only know the terrain more intimately than higher-level decision-makers; they are also more likely to comply with rules and regulations they have helped to devise than with prescriptions that are imposed from above. Analysts have been quick to point out that in most cases of comanagement the formal authority to make decisions continues to rest with higher-level agencies. But when they are effective, co-management bodies typically succeed by fostering a sense of legitimacy and a feeling among resource users that their voices are being heard in decision-making processes. Comanagement arrangements can work at a variety of levels. In the case of caribou that migrate across the international boundary between Alaska and the Yukon, there is even a mechanism joining local users and those responsible for international cooperation.[23] No one regards comanagement as a panacea; a combination of factors determines success in specific cases. Still, this is an approach to multilevel governance that deserves serious consideration in a variety of settings.

Adjudication

Turning to the courts or some other form of third-party adjudication offers a very different approach to addressing matters of multilevel governance. In the United States strategies of this sort are particularly prominent in addressing issues of air and water pollution. A number of states took the Environmental Protection Agency to court, for instance, over the question of whether greenhouse gases are pollutants as defined in the Clean Air Act Amendments of 1990 and won an affirmative ruling on the matter from the Supreme Court. Conversely, the Court ruled against a number of states in a case in which the states argued that the nuisance doctrine should apply to air pollution, thus giving them the authority to regulate greenhouse gas emissions regardless of the (in)action of the federal government. The judgment relied, in part, on the argument that federal authority to deal with this issue under the Clean Air Act Amendments of 1990 preempts any use of the nuisance doctrine on the part of individual states.[24] Conversely, states sometimes take the

EPA to court on the grounds that it is exceeding its authority in attempting to impose environmental regulations on state governments. A current case involves resistance to efforts on the part of the federal government to force states to apply national standards relating to emissions of greenhouse gases.[25] This approach too is not a panacea in addressing issues of multilevel governance; the confrontational nature of adjudication runs almost directly counter to the search for legitimacy and a sense of inclusiveness that animates efforts to devise comanagement regimes. Further, the use of the courts to sort out issues of multilevel governance is much less relevant in societies where resorting to litigation plays a more limited role than it does in the United States. Nevertheless, adjudication certainly belongs in the tool kit of those seeking to address matters of multilevel governance.

Legislation

A fourth family of strategies encompasses those that seek to address matters of multilevel governance through legislative measures or even the introduction of amendments to national constitutions. In the United States, for instance, this is always sensitive terrain due to disagreements regarding the interpretation of the Tenth Amendment to the Constitution dealing with states' rights and the various arguments that the federal government has deployed over the years to justify expanding its authority over issues involving natural resources and the environment. Yet the federal government has often succeeded in enhancing its role in this realm by passing legislation extending its authority into new areas. A particularly prominent example involves the enactment of the National Environmental Policy Act (NEPA) of 1969 and the steps that have been taken to implement the provisions of the act over time.[26] NEPA set the federal government up as a powerful player in addressing environmental issues, with the capacity to take action regarding issues reaching all the way down to the local level. Among other things, the act led to the creation of the Environmental Protection Agency, the establishment of the Council on Environmental Quality, and the development of the requirement to produce environmental impact statements in all cases involving "significant" federal actions. These initiatives have pro-voked intense opposition, fueled in considerable part by antagonism toward the federal government's expanded authority over an area with regard to which the Constitution is silent. Yet today they form the backbone of a governance system that has produced a dramatic shift in the balance of power between the federal government and state governments with regard to environmental issues.

Conclusion

Vertical interplay between and among environmental regimes, treated for the most part as a matter of multilevel governance, has emerged as a topic of intense interest among those concerned with environmental governance. In part, this is a result of changing so-cioecological conditions. Today's environmental problems typically feature cross-level links. Climate change is a global problem whose solution requires a high level of international cooperation. But local actions are implicated as drivers of climate change, and the impacts of climate change will be felt at the local level. Partly, it is a conse-quence of shifts in the distribution of political authority. National governments have assumed increased authority to address environ-mental problems, though this is not a matter of simple reallocation in the sense that the growing role of national governments has re-sulted in a diminution of the authority of local and regional gov-ernments to address environmental issues.[27] The result is a more complex picture of multilevel governance, in which progress de-pends on finding ways to minimize conflict and even encourage synergy in cross-level interactions in which actors operating at dif-ferent levels seek not only to solve environmental problems but also to protect or enhance their own interests in the process.

Although I have separated them for purposes of analysis, vertical and horizontal interplay operate simultaneously and interact with one another. States struggle at the international level to alleviate tensions between the world trade regime and, for example, the regime created to protect biological diversity with regard to the regulation of genetically modified organisms. But key actors also wrestle with tensions between federal agencies and state agencies regarding farming practices and interstate commerce involving agricultural products. Similar remarks are in order regarding interactions between domestic and international actions designed to address the problem of climate change. There are no simple solutions to these challenges of interplay management. These interactions will be affected by clashes between alternative worldviews and by the efforts of a variety of nonstate actors—including both multinational corporations and nongovernmental organizations—as well as by the actions of governments operating at different levels of social organizations. Efforts to meet these challenges constitute the domain of what I call complex environmental governance.

Part III

Environmental Governance in the Anthropocene

CHAPTER SIX

THE GREAT ACCELERATION

LIVING IN A NO-ANALOGUE STATE

European visitors to the east coast of North America during the fifteenth and sixteenth centuries, such as John Cabot who arrived in 1497, often noted that cod were so abundant that those desiring to harvest them had only to lower a basket and scoop up the desired amount. As late as the 1880s T. H. Huxley, a prominent British scientist and well-known proponent of Darwin's theory of natural selection, asserted famously (though erroneously as it turned out) that "the cod fishery, the herring fishery, the pilchard fishery, the mackerel fishery, and probably all the great sea fisheries, are inexhaustible; that is to say, that nothing we do seriously affects the number of the fish."[1] Equally distinguished commentators expressed similar views regarding other natural resources. Until the waning days of the nineteenth century knowledgeable observers of human-environment relations were able to assert that humans lacked the capacity to disrupt large biophysical systems.

More recently we have come to understand that human actions can deplete or degrade specific stocks of fish, parcels of farmland, stands of trees, and other natural resources. This insight, based largely on experience with small-scale systems, soon triggered growing concerns about avoiding the tragedy of the commons and regulating the behavior of what we have come to think of as "roving bandits."[2] Toward the end of the nineteenth century and during the early decades of the twentieth century efforts to address these concerns led, among other things, to the development of the conservation movement, with its emphasis on applying scientific methods to improve understanding of the behavior of biophysical systems, pursuing the goal of maximizing sustainable yields in harvesting renewable resources, and organizing harvesting practices in such a way as to promote the quest for economic efficiency.[3]

In recent years our thinking about human-environment relations has undergone a profound transformation. We now focus on the human domination of ecosystems and see ourselves as living in the Anthropocene, a new era in planetary history marked by the growing role of human actions as driving forces all the way up to the level of the Earth System.[4] The sources of this radical growth in the impact of human actions lie in the familiar variables of population, affluence, and technology, captured in the well-known formula $I = PAT$.[5] What stands out in efforts to understand the onset of the Anthropocene is the observation that a large suite of socioeconomic and biophysical forces accelerated dramatically in the second half of the twentieth century. Taken together, we have come to think of these developments as constituting the Great Acceleration, a transformative event calling for rapid and radical changes in our analytic lenses and worldviews as we struggle to devise a basis for addressing issues of environmental governance under the conditions prevailing in this new era.[6]

In this chapter and the next I explore the Great Acceleration and its implications for the practice of environmental governance. This chapter proceeds in two steps. The first section provides a descriptive account of the Great Acceleration. Just what does this evocative phrase refer to, and what are the processes that have caused human actions to dominate the Earth System during the lifetimes of many people alive today? The second section then turns to a discussion of the implications for governance of the defining features of the Anthropocene, such as the increasing frequency of events that are nonlinear, abrupt, irreversible, and often nasty from the perspective of human well-being and social welfare. I leave an analysis of the adjustments in established practices needed to create and administer environmental and resource regimes that can operate effectively under these new conditions for consideration in chapter 7.

The Great Acceleration

There is nothing new about the transformative impacts of human actions on the biophysical systems with which they interact.[7] Some of these impacts have been largely unintentional and for the most part unforeseen by the human actors involved. There is substantial evidence, for example, that humans played a large but unintentional role in driving various species of megafauna (e.g., woolly mammoths, saber-toothed tigers) to extinction both in northern Eurasia and North America during the late Pleistocene ten to twenty thousand years BP. The inhabitants of Easter Island destroyed the island's trees, seemingly unaware of the dire consequences of their actions for long-term well-being of the island's human population.[8] Even more recent developments, like the destruction of the entire population of passenger pigeons and the decimation of the buffalo herds of North America during the nineteenth century, most likely belong to the category of unintended and unforeseen consequences of human actions.

Other large-scale impacts have resulted from human actions of a more intentional nature. Humans have made use of fire from an early stage to manage landscapes for productivity, to protect themselves from wild animals, and to prepare protein-rich food. The domestication of animals and the development of agriculture some eight to ten thousand years BP marked a major turning point in the capacity of humans to transform biophysical systems with far-reaching consequences. The onset of the industrial revolution in the eighteenth century triggered a new era in humans' capacity to make intentional changes in their biophysical environment.

The eighteenth and nineteenth centuries brought a pattern of human-environment relations, especially in the new world, providing textbook illustrations of the phenomenon aptly described as roving banditry.[9] Farmers cleared land for agriculture, used the land exhaustively, and abandoned their farms in search of new land farther to the west, leaving settlements after a period of intensive land use lasting no more than fifty to seventy-five years. Harvesters of wood products also simply stripped land of its original forest and then moved to the west in search of new forests to conquer, leaving vast areas of ruined forest in their wake. A similar pattern arose with regard to marine resources. Harvesters of oysters, clams, and mussels, for instance, exploited standing stocks with abandon, assuming that they could move from stock to stock indefinitely without any concern for conservation. In the United States public policies often encouraged this pattern of sequential depletion. National legislation, in such forms as the Homestead Act of 1862 and the Mining Act of 1872, rested on the proposition that the public domain should be transferred into the hands of private owners sooner rather than later and generally abetted the propensity of users to exploit natural resources with little thought to the long-term consequences.[10]

Concern about land degradation in Europe along with the closing of the frontier in the United States during the waning decades of the nineteenth century and the opening decades of the twentieth century triggered an initial wave of interest in developing explicit principles of resource management. Starting with the creation of new agencies—like the US Geological Survey, dedicated to mapping and documenting the full extent of the nation's natural resources—this wave of interest led both to the application of science to issues of resource management and to a series of initiatives aimed at preserving natural areas of special interest.[11] The results included developing new fields of study (e.g., sylviculture), establishing new educational facilities (e.g., the Yale School of Forestry), forming new public agencies (e.g., the US Forest Service), and launching long-term management programs for designated parts of the public domain (e.g., the national forests).[12]

Human Domination

Nevertheless, this emerging interest in resource management did little to slow the rising impact of anthropogenic drivers associated with population growth, increasing affluence, and new technologies. A particularly dramatic development in these terms is reflected in the growth curves displayed in figures 6.1a and 6.1b. Figure 6.1a documents a series of nonlinear shifts in anthropogenic forces starting around 1950. The curves showing the trends in human population and gross world product are relatively familiar. But note the concurrent shifts in a sizable suite of other factors, such as water use, fertilizer consumption, paper consumption, use

Figure 6.1a The Great Acceleration: Socioeconomic Trends

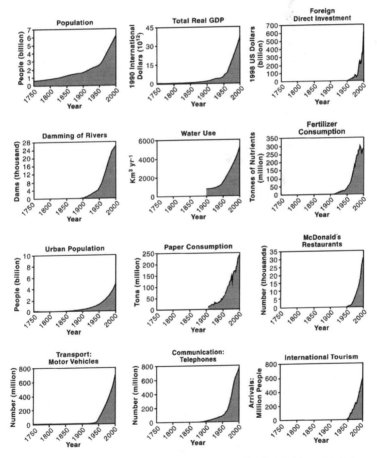

Source: International Geosphere-Biosphere Programme. Reprinted with permission.

of motor vehicles, and international tourism. Taken together, this suite of indicators provides compelling evidence of the occurrence of a phase shift or state change in the role of human actions as a dominant force in planetary terms. The overall effects are largely unintended and for the most part unforeseen, but this is neither here nor there when it comes to assessing the impacts of these anthropogenic forces on the Earth as a system.

Figure 6.1b includes a suite of indicators of biogeochemical trends that are correlated with these anthropogenic forces. Here too there is a sharp inflection around 1950. Whether we look at atmospheric, marine, or terrestrial systems, the pattern is much the same. It does not follow automatically that these changes are (fully) attributable to human actions, yet the links are evident in many cases, including atmospheric concentrations of carbon dioxide, stratospheric ozone depletion, transformation of land for human uses, destruction of tropical forests, and loss of biological diversity. The overall picture that emerges is not one of long-term development occurring on a steady basis; rather, it is the sharp nonlinear shift on a planetary scale starting around 1950 that has given rise to what we now refer to as the Great Acceleration.[13]

Some figures on specific manifestations of the human domination of the Earth System will serve to provide a concrete picture of this new world. The Earth's human population, which now stands at more than seven billion, showed its highest annual growth rates in the decades of the 1950s through the 1970s, peaking at 2.2 percent per year in 1963. Although it took 123 years for world's population to grow from one to two billion, the growth from six to seven billion occurred in just twelve years.[14] Humans have transformed about "50 percent of the world's ice-free land surface . . . and the land under cropping has doubled during the past century at the expense of forests, which declined by 20 percent during the same period."[15] Humans now appropriate for their own use more than 50 percent of available freshwater. Major rivers (e.g., the Colorado, Nile, and Yangtze) frequently run dry by the time they reach the coast, and humans are consuming water contained in large aquifers at a pace that far exceeds the recharge rate, effectively mining fossil water. The concentration of carbon dioxide in the Earth's

Figure 6.1b The Great Acceleration: Biophysical Trends

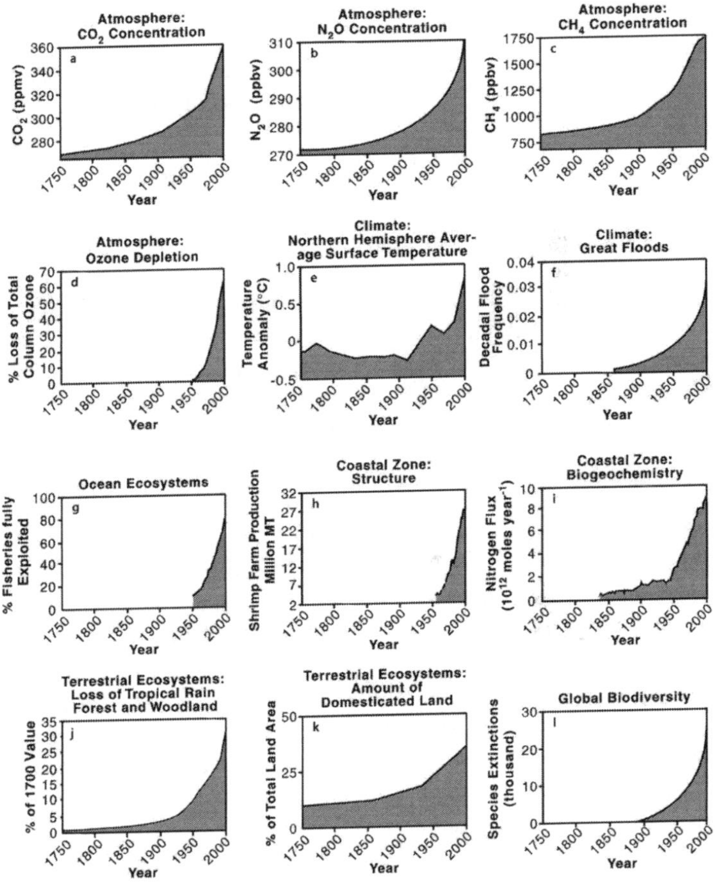

Source: International Geosphere-Biosphere Programme. Reprinted with permission.

atmosphere has increased from a preindustrial level of approximately 270ppm to the current level of about 392ppm, and the rate of increase is now around 2ppm per year. At present, "more nitrogen is . . . fixed synthetically and applied as agricultural fertilizers than is fixed naturally in all terrestrial ecosystems."[16] Among the results are a seasonal recurrence of large dead zones in the world's oceans and an unprecedented acidification of marine systems. Invasive species now move from place to place on a worldwide basis at unprecedented speeds. Overall, the "rates of species extinction are now on the order of 100 to 1000 times those before humanity's domination of the Earth."[17] The result is a loss of biological diversity on a scale that is now generally recognized as the sixth great extinction event in the Earth's history.

The Anthropocene

Taken together, these developments have triggered the onset of a new era in the Earth's history, in which human actions have emerged as the dominant force on a planetary scale. This era, now widely described as the Anthropocene as a way to differentiate it from the Holocene and to capture the idea of human domination, has propelled us into what scientists refer to as a *no-analogue state.*[18] What this means is that it is not helpful to compare this new era with previous eras in the Earth's history in an effort to understand the resultant planetary dynamics. One basic feature of the new era is already becoming clear: although the Holocene was a generally stable era that provided a benign setting for the development of human societies during the last ten thousand years, it is increasingly apparent that the "Earth is rapidly moving into a less biologically diverse, less forested, much warmer, and probably wetter and stormier state."[19] The Anthropocene will be a period of increased turbulence of a sort that will have far-reaching consequences for human well-being and social welfare. But what can we say about the characteristics of this new era that will require careful attention on the part of those seeking to govern human-environment relations in a sustainable manner?

Implications for Governance

The issues I have addressed in previous chapters in thinking first about simple environmental governance and then about complex environmental governance remain relevant. But the onset of the Anthropocene brings a number of new challenges into sharp relief.

In this section I identify and comment on these challenges under the following headings: (i) the management of human behavior, (ii) biophysical and socioeconomic teleconnections, (iii) tipping elements and tipping points, (iv) planetary boundaries, and (v) irreducible uncertainty.

Human Behavior

The critical challenge at this stage stems from the recognition that resource management in a world of human-dominated ecosystems must focus on efforts to manage or guide human behavior rather than on an effort to improve our knowledge of the behavior of biophysical systems. This is not to say that there is no need for improved knowledge in areas like fisheries science, soil science, sylviculture, climate science, and so forth. A particularly important direction in this realm arises from the idea of ecosystem-based management, with its emphasis on understanding how specific resources (e.g., fish, trees) fit into the dynamics of larger systems. Nevertheless, the era in which we could say "nothing we do seriously affects the number of fish," the condition of agricultural land, the composition of the atmosphere, and so forth is over. The crucial need now is to improve our ability to explain, predict, and steer human actions that have become powerful drivers of the course of human-environment relations. Several conditions make this challenge particularly difficult. One of these stems from the fact that there is incontrovertible evidence that individuals often behave in ways that cannot be explained in terms of the models of rational choice embedded in the logic of consequences.[20] Whether we are dealing with the inability of individuals to think carefully about the future consequences of actions taken today, their propensity to struggle to maintain unsustainable lifestyles, or their tendency to live in denial when it comes to issues like the onset of climate change, there is a critical need to supplement analyses based on models of rational choice with insights drawn from the fields of psychology, social psychology, and sociology.[21] Another, albeit related, factor has to do with the interactions among human actors, or what we generally think of in terms of the idea of collective action. Problems of collective action in the sense of situations in which interactive decision making leads to results that are undesirable for all parties concerned go far beyond the comparatively simple problem of the tragedy of the commons considered in chapter 1. Today we are faced with such problems on a global scale, as in the case of climate change, in which everyone's actions contribute to the problem, but no one has a sense of efficacy regarding their capacity individually to do anything about it.

How can we improve our understanding of these phenomena in a way that will help address issues of environmental governance? There is an understandable tendency to approach this topic as a matter of coupled human-natural systems and, in effect, to add another term to equations designed to illuminate the forces that determine the extent to which outcomes are sustainable. Although this is a natural and undoubtedly useful way to think about human-environment relations in the Anthropocene, it is far from clear whether it will provide a basis for effective governance in this new era. It seems likely that the Earth System, treated as a complex and dynamic socioecological system, will behave in ways that differ fundamentally from the behavior of this system during the Holocene.[22] The next three factors all involve efforts to unpack this observation.

Teleconnections

The concept of teleconnections, developed initially by atmospheric scientists, has come to refer to connections among remote elements of the Earth System that are unanticipated and surprising but turn out to play important roles in the dynamics of the system as a whole.[23] The link between the release of ozone-depleting substances in the midlatitudes of the northern hemisphere and the occurrence of a seasonal ozone hole over the high latitudes of the southern hemisphere is a prominent example. So are the links connecting anthropogenic emissions of carbon soot in the midlatitudes and (i) the melting of glaciers in the Himalayas, leading to sharp shifts in stream flows in the major rivers of Asia, and (ii) the recession of sea ice in the Arctic, leading to increased storm surges that are likely to force coastal communities to relocate under adverse circumstances. Yet another example involves the links between anthropogenic emissions of greenhouse gases and ocean acidification, leading to ecological effects like the degradation or destruction of coral reefs. The implications of this phenomenon for the practice of environmental governance are twofold. We must think of the Earth System in holistic terms; local and even regional perspectives on human-environment relations will no longer suffice. And we must be prepared to respond promptly and effectively to these unexpected connections even when they take us by surprise.

Tipping Elements

Another factor that surfaces in thinking about the Earth as a complex and dynamic socioecological system centers on the ideas of tipping elements and tipping points. Tipping points are thresholds where small perturbations can trigger transformative changes in the behavior of complex systems. Once a system passes such a point of no return, it will respond in a nonlinear fashion, moving toward some new state that differs more or less dramatically from the previous state. Analysts seeking to understand the Earth System have introduced the idea of tipping elements treated as "large-scale components of the Earth system that may pass a tipping point," and they have sought to compile a list of these elements together with the location of the point of no return in each case.[24] As figure 6.2 indicates, current thinking about this theme has drawn attention to a suite of tipping elements, ranging from the loss of sea ice in the Arctic to dieback of the Amazon rainforest and chaotic behavior of the Indian monsoon. The implications of this factor for environmental governance reinforce those identified in the preceding account of teleconnections. It takes very little to push a system operating in a critical zone past a point of no return. Yet decision-makers rarely factor such considerations into their thinking about human-environment relations, a fact that leads almost inevitably to a lack of preparation to respond promptly and effectively to occurrences such as the detection of the Antarctic ozone hole in 1984–1985, the collapse of Arctic sea ice in 2007, and the prospect of events like the sudden release of large quantities of methane now trapped in permafrost and methane hydrates.

126

Figure 6.2 Tipping Elements in the Earth System

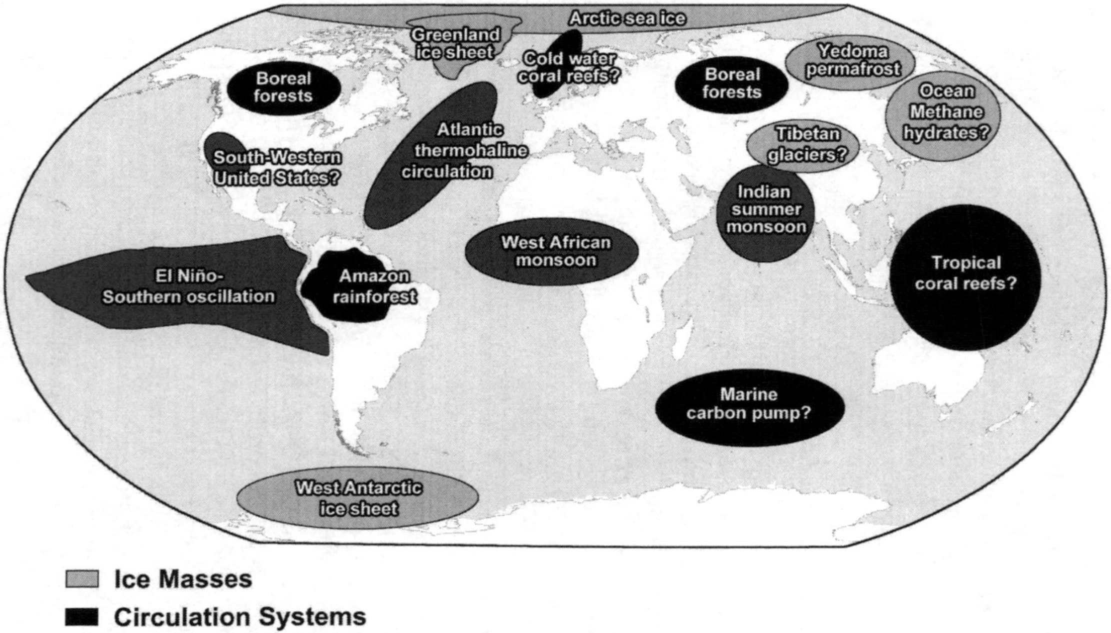

Ice Masses

Circulation Systems

Source: Timothy M. Lenton et al., "Tipping Elements in the Earth's Climate System," *Proceedings of the National Academy of Sciences* 105 [2008]: 1786–93. Reprinted with permission.

Planetary Boundaries

Recently, prominent members of the science community have introduced a new line of thinking about the Earth System based on the concept of planetary boundaries. The essential idea here is that we can identify a set of conditions that constitute a "safe operating space for humanity" and that movement beyond the boundaries of this space leads progressively to more and more dangerous conditions from the perspective of human well-being and social welfare.[25] So far, as portrayed in figure 6.3, these analysts have identified nine boundaries and provided some basis for developing quantitative measures of seven of them. At this time, they assert, human actions have pushed the system beyond the safe operating space with regard to three of these boundaries involving the nitrogen cycle, climate change, and the loss of biological diversity. The implications

Figure 6.3 Planetary Boundaries

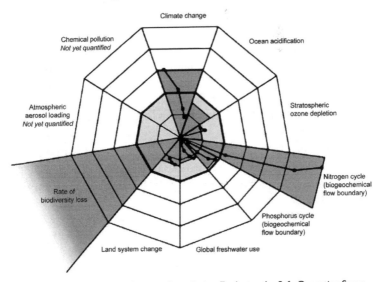

Source: J. Rockström et al., "Planetary Boundaries: Exploring the Safe Operating Space for Humanity," *Ecology and Society* 14, no. 2, art. 32, http://www.ecologyandsociety.org /vol14/iss2/art32/. Reprinted with permission.

of this line of thinking for environmental governance are straight-forward but profound: we must now engage in a concerted effort on a global scale to return to a safe operating space with regard to those boundaries we have already transgressed and to avoid moving out of the safe operating space with respect to the other boundaries. This argument does not presume to prescribe the mechanisms of governance that are needed to solve this problem, but it does constitute a wake-up call regarding the growing problem of fit between the characteristics of the challenges of environmental governance we now face and the properties of the environmental regimes we have put in place to address them.

Acting Under Uncertainty

Reflecting on the factors considered in this section so far, one major condition that has far-reaching implications for environmental governance stands out: we must find ways forward that provide a basis for acting under conditions of uncertainty. Not only is it hard to forecast the path of human behavior, especially in situations featuring collective action; it is also clear that our ability to foresee the trajectory of the Earth System treated as a complex and dynamic socioecological system will remain limited for the indefinite future. This is not to deny the value of continuing efforts to enhance our understanding of phenomena like tipping points and planetary boundaries. But there will be no avoiding the need to make choices about issues like emissions of greenhouse gases under conditions in which our capacity to assess the costs and benefits of different options—including the option of doing nothing—will be severely limited. Some may respond to this challenge by promoting the idea of the precautionary principle, but this is not a satisfactory response in situations in which there are persuasive reasons to believe that what is needed now are decisive steps to move us off the path of business as usual, at least in cases like climate change and the loss of biological diversity. Some other basis for identifying and weighing the choices available to us both individually and collectively must supersede the present disjointed procedures in which environmental governance is handled through decentralized and typically ad hoc procedures.

Conclusion

The argument of this chapter does not supersede the account of environmental governance developed in the preceding chapters dealing with simple environmental governance and complex environmental governance. If anything, dilemmas of collective action and problems of environmental side effects will loom larger as we move progressively into an era when human actions have become dominant forces that drive biophysical processes on a planetary scale. As those who emphasize the idea of sustainable development in contrast to environmental protection have made clear, moreover, we face a situation now in which interactions between economic and social processes and the state of the biophysical environment are major determinants of human well-being and social welfare.[26] There is no way to make real progress in addressing issues like climate change or the loss of biological diversity without making progress in meeting basic human needs, such as those articulated in the UN's Millennium Declaration adopted in 2000 (discussed in detail in the next chapter).[27]

What is the way forward under these conditions? How can and should we respond to the challenges of the Anthropocene in a manner that is forceful enough to make a difference in moving us toward sustainability on a planetary scale yet pragmatic enough to stand a chance of being adopted and implemented in global society as we know it today? This is a set of questions that now animates a concerted effort to build a body of knowledge dealing with earth system governance.[28] The next chapter explores a set of steps relating to environmental governance developed with these questions in mind.

CHAPTER SEVEN
THE SUSTAINABILITY TRANSITION

GOVERNING DYNAMIC SYSTEMS

The Great Acceleration has emerged as a game changer with regard to environmental governance. Solving collective-action problems, addressing environmental side effects, accounting for institutional interplay, and coming to terms with multilevel governance all remain critical pieces of the puzzle in efforts to create effective environmental governance systems. But now it has become essential to integrate three additional factors into the mix in forming and implementing regimes to guide human-environment relations. One factor centers on the need to focus on the Earth System as the proper unit of analysis in crafting the terms of environmental regimes. This is the essential insight of the line of thinking we now characterize as *Earth System governance*.[1] A second, equally important consideration arises from the fact that we are entering a period of increased *turbulence in large socioecological systems*. We must devise arrangements that can perform well in a world whose dynamics are often nonlinear, generally irreversible, and frequently abrupt.[2] Under these conditions there is nothing to be gained from putting off taking steps to address large-scale environmental issues in the hope that a little extra time will allow us to avoid the need to make decisions under high levels of uncertainty. The third factor arises from the need to embed efforts to address environmental concerns within the larger discourse of *sustainable development*. Admittedly, sustainable development is a desired outcome that is difficult to define operationally, much less to measure in the form of an agreed-upon suite of quantifiable indicators that makes tracking progress in this realm possible.[3] Nevertheless, it is abundantly clear that residents of the developing world will not tolerate a situation in which we devote ourselves to coming to grips with problems like climate change or the loss of biological diversity at the expense of concerted efforts to improve the well-being of large numbers of people struggling to emerge from poverty and desiring to enjoy the benefits of more affluent lifestyles.

This chapter tackles this array of issues in three steps. The first section identifies a collection of strategies that will prove helpful to those endeavoring to form and administer environmental regimes that perform well in turbulent times. Focusing on strategies emphasizing anticipation as well as adaptation, this discussion makes it clear that the requirements for creating effective governance systems in turbulent times differ significantly from those that suffice to ensure success in more stable settings. The next section raises the question of whether we need a new environmental order or, to put it another way, a new contract between humans and nature to govern human-environment relations in a world of human-dominated ecosystems. We are well past the time when observers could conclude that "nothing we do seriously affects the number of fish" or any other significant form of natural capital.[4] But we have yet to develop a set of basic principles applicable to this new era of human-environment relations that can provide a solid foundation on which to build a collection of environmental and resources regimes dealing with a host of concrete issues. The final section then turns to a discussion of the links between efforts to address the challenges of environmental governance and a variety of other values that are important to human communities. With all due respect to those who think of climate change and the loss of biological diversity as the paramount issues of our times, there is no escaping the desire of humans, both individually and collectively, to pursue a variety of other goals. Particularly compelling in this context are the concerns for human dignity and social welfare captured in the Millennium Development Goals.

Governance in Turbulent Times

The defining features of the Holocene/Anthropocene transition are the onset of human domination of the Earth's ecosystems and, at the same time, a shift from benign conditions in biophysical terms to an unsettled era characterized by fluctuations that are pronounced in terms of both scope and speed. As figure 7.1 shows, the Holocene was a remarkably settled period with regard to temperature; other indicators confirm this overall picture of a world conducive to the human enterprise. Although it is difficult to forecast long-term trends in indicators like temperature, there is broad consensus among scientists on the proposition that we are now moving into a period of increased volatility. What are the implications of the resultant turbulence in the Earth System for environmental governance? This section discusses three sets of strategies

Figure 7.1 Past Temperature Variation

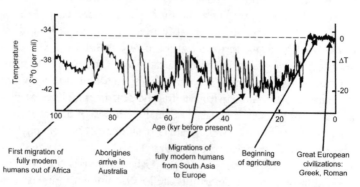

Source: J. Rockström et al., "Planetary Boundaries: Exploring the Safe Operating Space for Humanity," Ecology and Society 14, no. 2, art. 32, http://www.ecologyandsociety.org /vol14/iss2/art32/. Reprinted with permission.

that come into focus during efforts to steer human-environment relations in turbulent times: (i) harnessing reflexivity, (ii) enhancing adaptive capacity, and (iii) coping with uncertainty.

Harnessing Reflexivity

Reflexive systems are those in which the actors are able to respond consciously to recent events, anticipate future developments, and adjust their behavior on the basis of expectations about the course of events in the future. Although foresight is a necessary condition for efforts to make midcourse corrections intended to take advantage of emerging opportunities or avoid prospective dangers, it is not a sufficient condition for success in these terms. For one thing, anticipation can trigger positive feedback processes that lead to dangerous spirals, or what are commonly known as self-fulfilling prophecies.[5] Classic examples feature runs on banks and stock market crashes following a loss of confidence on the part of depositors or investors. But environmental examples are easy to identify as well. Think of situations in which appropriators rush to capture the last remaining units of a common pool resource or engage in a race to the bottom by lowering environmental standards to prevent industries from picking up and moving to locations with laxer regulatory standards. Alternatively, anticipatory responses may produce chaotic situations in which actors rush from one response to another in a desperate search for effective ways to protect themselves from anticipated threats to their welfare. Coastal communities that swing back and forth between efforts to reinforce their sea walls and developing plans to relocate in the face of anticipated rises in sea levels as a consequence of climate change exemplify this case.

So reflexivity is not always a beneficial phenomenon from the perspective of those concerned with human well-being and social welfare. There are reasons to believe that human-dominated ecosystems may prove more volatile than those in which the impacts of human actions are more limited.[6] But let us set aside these dangerous aspects of reflexivity for the moment and ask about the possibility of negative feedback processes, or processes in which the anticipation of problems leads to the development of countercyclical measures or corrections designed to reduce the probability that current actions will lead to undesirable outcomes.

The key issues here concern when to respond to anticipated occurrences, what response strategies to select, and how to coordinate responses to large-scale developments. The issue of when to respond can be tricky. It does not make sense to overreact or to react in a hasty or precipitous manner, taking vigorous steps when the first sign of trouble appears on the horizon and before the nature of the problem is properly understood. However, there is a natural tendency to carry on with business as usual, a tendency that can and often does delay responses until it is too late to make a real difference in heading off a problem. This is precisely the dilemma we face today with regard to climate change. Should we be taking vigorous action now to prevent or ameliorate the changes in the Earth's climate system expected to flow from increases in atmospheric concentrations of greenhouse gases? If so, should we focus our attention on mitigation or the effort to prevent the occurrence of climate change, even if this means ignoring or deemphasizing adaptation or the effort to minimize future impacts of climate change by taking steps to reduce our vulnerability to the effects of climate change? As this case suggests, it is particularly difficult to launch anticipatory responses that make a difference in situations in which success depends on coordinating the efforts of a large number of individual actors, and there is reason to believe that the opportunity costs associated with effective responses will be large.

Anticipatory responses that prove effective in solving or deflecting emerging problems are unlikely in situations in which the relevant actors lack a sense of efficacy. It is one thing to make an effort to reduce your vulnerability by buying a more fuel-efficient car when you expect gasoline prices to rise in the future or renovating your home to improve efficiency when you expect the price of electricity or heating oil to rise; it is another to invest time and energy in efforts to reduce greenhouse gas emissions at the national or even the international level in order to avoid the occurrence of climate change altogether. The issue here is a matter of personal efficacy. Even those who are deeply concerned about the prospect that we are headed toward severe disruption of the Earth's climate system are apt to feel a lack of efficacy when it comes to making changes at the societal level needed to avoid this development. As Kari Norgaard has aptly observed, individuals who feel there is little they can do to reduce the probability of climate change occurring tend to live in denial, carrying on with business as usual even though they know perfectly well that problems like climate change may erode their well-being in the future.[7] It follows that those who want to harness reflexivity so as to head off looming environmental problems before they occur or become severe must find ways to bolster the sense of efficacy of those whose actions they are endeavoring to change.

Enhancing Adaptive Capacity

Anticipatory responses are designed to prevent the occurrence of environmental problems or at least to limit their impacts. Whatever the effectiveness of such responses, however, it makes sense under the unsettled or turbulent conditions of the Anthropocene to think about enhancing adaptive capacity or the ability to cope with the impacts of environmental changes that do occur in such a way as to minimize losses of human well-being or social welfare. Some forms of adaptation are easy to identify and relatively straightforward to pursue. In periods of extreme volatility in the stock market, for instance, prudent investors are likely to diversify their investments and shift the balance in their portfolios between equities and other financial instruments in order to protect their assets and position themselves to respond in a flexible manner to developments that are hard to anticipate. Farmers faced with sizable swings in temperatures and rainfall that are impossible to forecast far enough in advance to make a difference may seek to enhance their capacity to adapt to changes by adopting cropping practices that are easy to adjust or even change in more drastic ways on relatively short notice.

When it comes to enhancing adaptive capacity in the face of the kinds of environmental issues we now face in the wake of the Great Acceleration, however, a number of tricky issues arise. For one thing, it is not cheap to enhance adaptive capacity. Such strategies are apt to entail more or less substantial costs in such forms as missed opportunities to make gains from investments in equities or to profit from concentrating on high-value crops, a matter of considerable importance especially for individuals and societies that find it hard to spare resources for initiatives that may turn out to have been unnecessary. For another, individual members of relevant groups are likely to differ with regard to their assessment of the relative merits of various strategies designed to enhance adaptive capacity. This may not be a problem for the efforts of individuals to strengthen their adaptive capacity; they can make their own decisions about such matters, and the consequences are not likely to have far-reaching impacts on social welfare. But the prospect of diverse preferences regarding adaptation strategies can become a serious stumbling block in situations in which there is a need for collective decisions about what steps to take.

The case of climate change is instructive here as well as in the discussion of anticipatory responses. As we start to experience the impacts of climate change in such forms as temperature increases, wetter or drier seasons, and sea-level rise causing coastal erosion, attention has begun to shift toward adaptation in contrast to mitigation.[8] But whereas mitigation is simply a matter of reducing greenhouse gas emissions (or finding ways to withdraw such gases already in the atmosphere), adaptation is a far more complex challenge, in which strategies that make sense for one country or even a region within a country are not relevant for other countries or regions. And even when we focus on a single country or region, the feasibility of launching effective adaptation strategies is hard to assess. The difficulty of mobilizing the resources needed to undertake adaptation measures is another barrier to effective action in this realm. Many of the societies most vulnerable to the impacts of climate change are not in a position to spare the resources needed to enhance their adaptive capacities significantly. The wealthy countries have made promises about providing funds to those in need of help in this endeavor. The 2009 Copenhagen Accord, for example, states that the wealthy countries intend to provide $30 billion to address problems of climate change during the 2009–2012 period and to ramp up funding for this purpose to $100 billion per year by 2020.[9] At this writing, however, there is little evidence that the wealthy countries will make good on this promise, especially if their efforts are expected to take the form of what are known as "new and additional" funds. What is more, those who have studied the track record of development assistance in such forms as foreign aid are skeptical both about the absorptive capacity of recipient countries and about avoiding incompetence and corruption on the part of those who administer such aid. Enhancing adaptive capacity is critical, but doing so to ameliorate the impacts of specific environmental problems is easier said than done.

Coping with Uncertainty

A third family of strategies that come into focus in turbulent times involve methods of coping with uncertainty. There is always a case for investing resources in efforts to reduce uncertainty, but it is clear that the turbulent conditions of the Anthropocene will necessitate decision making under uncertainty with respect to important issues no matter how much time and energy we expend on such efforts. Doing nothing is effectively a decision to carry on with business as usual, an option that may turn out to be particularly inappropriate under the conditions prevailing today and likely to prevail during the foreseeable future.[10] What are the alternatives? Some analysts suggest that the way forward is to adopt some version of the precautionary principle. But what does this strategy entail in practice? As experience in the realm of national security suggests, employing some form of "worst-case analysis" does not necessarily ensure success in avoiding destructive sequences of events, and in any case, it will prove prohibitively expensive for all but the wealthiest societies. This enhances the appeal of the idea of "safe operating spaces," as articulated by those who have developed the analysis of planetary boundaries, or the idea of erecting environmental "guardrails," as developed by those who urge us to err on the side of safety with regard to matters like operationalizing the goal of avoiding "dangerous anthropogenic interference" in the Earth's climate system.[11] Yet none of these procedures offers a straightforward way ahead in confronting the uncertainties of the Anthropocene.

A number of alternative approaches to governance that do make sense in this setting are coming into focus now. It is appealing to opt for relatively short commitment periods or include sunset provisions in crafting governance systems so that it is comparatively easy to make adjustments as we learn more about the behavior of the socioecological systems underlying environmental issues. There is a good case for framing policy initiatives in this context in experimental terms in the sense of putting in place at the outset procedures designed to monitor the results of such initiatives closely and make it possible to adjust or reconfigure the attributes of regimes on the basis of the insights generated through such processes. There may be cases in which it is possible to devise insurance schemes dealing with environmental threats, although there are good reasons to think carefully about the problem of moral hazard in any effort that reduces the extent to which potential victims worry about the probable consequences of environmental changes. There is much to be said for the usefulness of what Amos Tversky and Daniel Kahneman have described as heuristics and rules of thumb.[12] Such rules offer relatively simple guidelines for selecting prudent courses of action in situations in which uncertainty is a prominent feature of the landscape and there is little prospect that scientific consensus regarding the issues at stake will emerge during the foreseeable future. A good rule of thumb with regard to matters of environmental governance, for example, is to think through the pros and cons of options for (re)forming governance systems in advance in order to be prepared to take advantage of windows of opportunity when change becomes feasible, even if there is no way to anticipate when such windows will open and how long they are likely to remain open.

A New Environmental Order?

There is much to be said at this stage for reexamining and perhaps reforming the deep structure or the constitutive foundations on which environmental regimes rest in the light of the conditions prevailing in the wake of the Great Acceleration. Three factors seem particularly important as reasons to undertake such an assessment. We must think in terms of the Earth System in the sense that it is no longer appropriate to limit our attention to national—much less subnational—systems in creating and implementing effective environmental regimes. We must reckon with the fact that we are operating in a world of human-dominated ecosystems in the sense that anthropogenic forces taken together now play a large role in determining the trajectory of socioecological systems all the way from the local to the planetary level. And we must grasp the significance of the observation that these systems are subject to changes that are often nonlinear, abrupt, and irreversible. In short, we must take a close look at the overarching implications for governance arising from the Holocene/Anthropocene transition.[13]

Deep Structure

All too often observers respond to such challenges by recommending organizational reforms, such as upgrading the UN Environment Programme (UNEP) into a specialized agency in the UN System or a body similar to the WTO in the issue domain of trade rather than asking whether we need to be thinking about changes in the deep structure of the current system. In thinking about deep structure the first step is to recognize that environmental governance is more about guiding human actors' behavior than it is about managing biophysical systems and that guiding human behavior is at least as much a matter of the logic of appropriateness as it is a matter of the logic of consequences.[14] There is no doubt about the efficacy of incentive mechanisms at the operational level; human actors do pay attention to the benefits and costs associated with different responses to environmental regulations. But at a deeper level we need to focus on the role of worldviews, values, and norms as determinants of the course of human-environment relations.[15] To create environmental governance systems that are effective in dealing with specific problems, we need to foster an awareness that humans are parts of the Earth System rather than outside actors, promote an ethic of stewardship in evaluating the consequences of human actions, and cultivate norms that emphasize the importance of conservation rather than consumptive uses of natural capital. Human actors who accept these principles as a point of departure will think about the relative merits of different options in a way that differs sharply from the calculations of those who focus exclusively on the benefits to be derived from exploiting natural resources and ecosystem services.

Linkages Across Levels

Similarly, there is a need to acknowledge the strength of linkages across levels of social organization in crafting the provisions of environmental governance systems. In modern times we have tended to focus on carving out separate and distinct spheres of authority for actors operating at different levels of social organization. Local governments have guarded jealously their authority over issues like zoning and the promulgation of building codes. National governments pay attention to matters like regulating interstate commerce and extending national jurisdiction over coastal waters. International arrangements are limited to those that states are willing to accept voluntarily in the form of conventions, treaties, executive agreements, and so forth. The emphasis throughout is on the allocation of authority among governments operating at different levels and on the resolution of controversies over initiatives likely to have the effect of shifting the prevailing allocation of authority.[16] This way of thinking is antithetical to what is needed to address environmental problems effectively under the conditions prevailing in the Anthropocene. Local actions (e.g., emissions of greenhouse gases, destruction of wetlands of importance to threatened species) can produce global consequences; global actions (e.g., the mobilization of funds designed to underwrite efforts to adapt to climate change) can make a difference at the local level. What is needed now is a way of thinking about governance that emphasizes the importance of building collaborative and mutually beneficial coalitions across levels of social organization rather than battling over the allocation of authority among governments operating at different levels. This is not simply a matter of adopting the principle of subsidiarity, which emphasizes the desirability of delegating authority to the lowest level of government with the capacity to address specific problems. Rather, the need is to adopt principles that stress the importance of multilevel governance or the development of bottom-up and top-down measures that are mutually supportive.

Institutional Agility

None of these measures will prove effective in solving the environmental problems arising today in the absence of governance systems able to respond in a nimble fashion to changes that are increasingly likely to be nonlinear, abrupt, and irreversible. This is a matter of particular concern in settings where domestic legislatures are paralyzed by ideological battles among unyielding adversaries and international bodies are slow to reach meaningful conclusions due to a need to arrive at consensus among large numbers of actors whose interests are highly diverse. The resultant disconnect between the need to respond agilely to fast-moving environmental issues and the difficulty of assembling winning coalitions in support of creating effective governance systems constitutes one of the overriding challenges facing those striving to develop solutions to a range of environmental problems such as climate change, the loss of biological diversity, desertification, the destruction of forests, the depletion of ocean resources, and the spread of pollution on a large scale.

However, there are some promising signs of efforts to address this challenge in specific arenas. The ability of the Meeting of the Parties to the Montreal Protocol on ozone-depleting substances to make decisions regarding the acceleration of phase-out schedules for specific chemicals that do not require ratification on the part of individual member countries to take effect, for instance, is a step in the right direction.[17] So also is the effort unfolding under the auspices of the Convention on Biological Diversity to forge agreement on the need to increase the size of areas accorded some sort of protected status.[18] Desirable as they are, however, these are modest steps that are limited to the activities of environmental regimes dealing with specific issues; they do not add up to a shift in the deep structure of environmental governance capable of changing the contours of the playing field for initiatives dealing with a wide range of more specific environmental problems.

Promoting Change

The emergence of a new environmental order based on these principles of stewardship, multilevel governance, and the need for institutional agility would make a profound difference for the efforts of those working at the operational level and struggling with issues like developing specific multilateral environmental agreements (e.g., the UN Framework Convention on Climate Change), strengthening UNEP, and articulating an appropriate role for the UN Commission on Sustainable Development (UNCSD). But how can we nurture movement toward such changes in the constitutive foundations of environmental governance? There is no simple answer to this question. One approach that is worthy of serious consideration emphasizes the role of global conferences like the 1972 UN Conference on the Human Environment and the 1992 UN Conference on Environment and Development. The 1972 conference played an important role in adding environmental concerns to the international agenda along with established issue domains like peace and security, economic development, and human rights. The 1992 conference brought the idea of sustainable development to the attention of policy-makers worldwide as a framework for thinking about human-environment relations. But these meetings, occurring during the midst of the Great Acceleration, did not succeed in putting in place a new environmental order of the sort under consideration here. This is not to denigrate the role of conference diplomacy with regard to the challenge of reforming constitutive principles that are deeply rooted in the history of thinking about human-environment relations, but more is needed now to address this challenge.

An alternative line of attack on this issue suggests that we will make more progress by reprogramming specific mechanisms like UNEP and the UNCSD and looking to these developments as a means of shifting worldviews, values, and norms in a manner that, over time, will produce significant changes in constitutive principles. A particularly interesting development in this regard is the effort to upgrade UNEP.[19] One of the threads embedded in this effort calls for establishing a World Environment Organization (WEO) based, at least in part, on the model of the WTO in the field of trade. The

WTO is one of the principal keepers of the constitutive principles of embedded liberalism, a worldview embracing free trade together with a modest level of regulatory intervention and public support coming from governments. There are signs that this worldview is fraying and may become increasingly tattered under the economic and political conditions emerging today. Nonetheless, the fact that the various elements of the international trade regime rest on a coherent worldview is a source of this regime's strength. A question that arises here is whether creating a WEO could change the way we address human-environment relations in the absence of a similarly coherent worldview and whether such an organization could play a role itself in encouraging such a shift in the deep structure of human-environment relations.

Although there is no simple answer to this question, the history of the trade regime is instructive in thinking about the matter.[20] The planned International Trade Organization, embodied in the terms of the Havana Charter negotiated during the 1947 UN Conference on Trade and Employment, never materialized due in considerable part to the lack of consensus on the constitutive principles underlying the proposed arrangement. What emerged in its place was the General Agreement on Tariffs and Trade (GATT), a considerably less ambitious exercise in international governance. The WTO itself did not come into existence until 1995 in the wake of the Uruguay Round of trade negotiations. With respect to principles governing human-environment relations, we may well be closer to the conditions prevailing in 1947 in contrast to 1995 with respect to international trade. This is not intended to put a damper on the visions of those who advocate creating a WEO, but it does suggest that there is farther to go in making the shift to a new environmental order than many backers of the proposed WEO are able or willing to acknowledge.

Environmental Governance in Context

To this point I have focused more or less exclusively on environmental governance and sought to understand the implications of the Great Acceleration for the creation and administration of effective environmental governance systems. But environmental problems do not exist in a vacuum. Human actors have other, sometimes more pressing matters on their minds; a variety of economic and political considerations circumscribe their capacity to respond to environmental challenges. Although those whose thinking is shaped by the onset of the Anthropocene are apt to treat problems like climate change as the great issue of our time, many policy-makers are more concerned with immediate problems like lifting people in the bottom billion out of poverty and addressing urgent matters of public health. In this section I turn to matters of development, globalization, and geopolitics and comment briefly on their implications for environmental governance.

The Millennium Development Goals

Poverty, along with a host of related issues involving food security, public health, and education, remains a paramount concern for many policy-makers in a world of seven billion people now expected to grow to more than ten billion before leveling off at the end of this century. As articulated in the UN Millennium Declaration adopted in September 2000, this concern has become a prominent item on the international agenda captured in the Millennium Development Goals (MDGs), a series of eight broad objectives with a target date for fulfillment of 2015 (encapsulated in figure 7.2).[21] From some points of view the MDGs are fully compatible with efforts to create or strengthen environmental governance systems. Controlling climate change, protecting biological diversity, and preventing desertification, for instance, are all matters of high priority from the perspective of those working to fulfill the MDGs. Yet there are tensions between the two agendas as well. Those located in the Global South, who are struggling to address immediate problems of food security, clean water, and adequate sanitation facilities in developing countries, often regard problems of climate change and biological diversity as distant concerns of interest to affluent populations in the North. And the knowledge that policy agendas are always crowded, making real progress in addressing multiple issues simultaneously difficult, reinforces these tensions.[22]

Figure 7.2 Millennium Development Goals

After UNDP.

The struggle to fulfill the MDGs has several implications for those concerned with environmental governance. In cases such as climate change, where there is no possibility of success in the absence of meaningful participation on the part of countries like Brazil, Russia, India, China, and South Africa (the so-called BRICS), progress will depend on generating a sense that environmental regimes are based on principles of environmental equity or justice. There is no way to draw these countries into effective participation in environmental regimes without taking steps to acknowledge their concerns about this matter. This means that wealthy northern countries will have to demonstrate that they are serious about adopting the principle of common but differentiated responsibilities in connection with specific regimes and recognize that it is physically impossible to bring the standard of living for seven billion people up to the level that the residents of the advanced industrial countries now enjoy. If predictions about the dramatic rise in the number of environmental refugees (i.e., people living involuntarily outside their country of origin as a result of environmental conditions) prove correct, the pressure on wealthy northern countries to respond in some significant way to the problem of environmental justice will become acute.[23]

Globalization

Related to this concern are issues arising from what is commonly labeled globalization, an umbrella term that refers to a suite of economic, social, and technological processes that are leading to a tighter integration of the socioeconomic components of the Earth System. In some respects this development constitutes part of the problem when it comes to environmental governance. Globalization plays a significant role in enhancing international trade, stimulating economic growth in the far corners of the world, and spreading forms of consumerism that entail high levels of material consumption. To the extent that these forces prevail, pressures on biophysical systems will continue to mount in ways that threaten to overcome the effects of environmental governance systems on a variety of fronts.

However, in the event that major actors take initiatives leading to the development of what is commonly called a green economy, globalization could become a positive force.[24] Although the term is imprecise, the idea of a green economy centers on developing productive systems that minimize destruction associated with consumptive uses of natural capital (e.g., the extraction of fossil fuels, the degradation of productive land, the mining of groundwater) and have the effect of reorienting conceptions of human well-being and social welfare away from materialistic lifestyles and toward more sustainable ones. Under these circumstances the integrative features of globalization would serve to spread this nonlinear change in values and norms to all corners of the world at a pace much more rapid than would have been possible even a few decades ago. It is not clear that the requirements of coming to terms with environmental problems will become a major—much less a decisive—force in bringing about a turn toward a global green economy, but the advent of a green economy could well prove decisive for efforts to solve major environmental problems like climate change. At a minimum it is clear that there are strong links between the environmental and the economic challenges we now face; real progress will require strategies that address the two challenges at the same time.

Geopolitical Shifts

Another piece of this puzzle centers on geopolitics, or the distribution of political power in both its hard and soft forms in the international system. Two large trends in this realm have important implications for efforts to address environmental problems. The period the Great Acceleration covers coincides largely with the era of US dominance as a global power. The United States played the leading role in creating the UN System in the aftermath of World War II, but the shift of the United States from the role of pusher to that of laggard in the realm of environmental affairs—starting with the law of the sea negotiations in the 1970–1980s and accelerating with the rise of climate change and biodiversity on the international agenda in the 1990s—has emerged as a stumbling block for those working to enhance environmental governance. Today we are witnessing a pronounced shift in geopolitical terms, as China, India, and Brazil are emerging as great powers, and the power of Europe as well as North America is waning at least in relative terms. Success in dealing with issues like climate change and the loss of biodiversity now will require buy-in on the part of these emerging great powers. Whether this is good or bad news from the point of view of environmental protection and sustainable development remains to be seen, but no account of environmental governance makes sense in the absence of a consideration of this trend.[25]

The other geopolitical trend centers on the rise of nonstate actors and the growing role of global civil society. Exaggerating this development would be a mistake; states are not about to lose their grip as the most important actors in world affairs. No effort to come to terms with issues like climate change and the loss of biological diversity can succeed without active participation on the part of key states. Nevertheless, it is difficult to see ways to address these problems successfully in the coming decades without devising procedures to draw multinational corporations and large nongovernmental organizations into the process of regime building. The result will be a growing need for more complex governance systems.[26] The simple model, featuring multilateral environmental agreements followed by suitable regulatory arrangements put in place by individual member states so as to ensure compliance on the part of domestic actors, is no longer sufficient. This opens up opportunities for nonstate actors to create private environmental regimes in such forms as the Forest Stewardship Council and the Marine Stewardship Council.[27] But there is no basis for assuming that we are entering an era in which it will be possible to bypass states in devising effective environmental regimes. For the foreseeable future mixed systems often featuring more or less intricate regime complexes will be the order of the day for those seeking to create governance systems that can solve major environmental problems.[28]

Conclusion

Making a transition to sustainability under the conditions prevailing in the Anthropocene will require innovation in the realm of environmental governance. Strategies involving efforts to harness reflexivity, enhance adaptive capacity, and cope with uncertainty can all play roles in addressing the need for governance in turbulent times. But the combination of human domination of the Earth's ecosystems and the economic and political changes now unfolding on a global scale requires a reexamination of the deep structure or constitutive foundations of environmental governance that moves beyond the level of adjusting the terms of specific arrangements dealing with issues like climate change or tinkering with existing organizations like UNEP. It would be highly undesirable to put off this exercise on the grounds that we must deal with other issues first or wait for the development of new knowledge to reduce uncertainty regarding issues like climate change. As the participants in the Nobel Laureate Symposium on Global Sustainability meeting in Stockholm in May 2011 put it: "We are the first generation facing the evidence of global change. It therefore falls upon us to change our relationship with the planet in order to tip the scales towards a sustainable world for future generations."[29]

Conclusion
Making Environmental
Governance Work

What can the analysis of environmental governance contribute to efforts to solve current problems like climate change, the loss of biological diversity, or the emergence of tensions between international environmental regimes and the trade regime? Can practitioners working to address these issues on the ground generate insights that enhance our understanding of environmental governance more generally? All too often there is a disconnect between the worlds of analysis and praxis with regard to environmental governance. Analysts seeking to explain or predict the formation and performance of environmental governance systems approach these concerns in general terms and have little or no contact with members of the policy community. As a result they are unable to produce insights regarding current issues that are helpful to practitioners. For their part practitioners seeking to create and administer regimes to address concrete problems have little or no contact with the world of those seeking to add to our knowledge of environmental regimes; they are too preoccupied with the details of specific issues to stand back and think about the relevance of the propositions that the analysts produce.

This disconnect is unfortunate for all parties concerned. It is a significant factor in accounting for the relatively high rate of failure in efforts to establish effective environmental regimes. What is needed to alleviate this situation and build up a body of usable knowledge about environmental governance? The answer to this question, I believe, lies in the development of a field of applied institutional analysis focused in the first instance on meeting the need for environmental governance but sensitive as well to insights derived from an examination of similarities and differences between environmental governance and governance in other issue domains.[1] In this concluding chapter I address this issue in two steps. The first section introduces what those interested in applied institutional analysis describe as *institutional diagnostics*. The essential idea here is to start with a careful examination of the characteristics of the problem to be solved and then to devise a governance system that fits the problem at hand rather than starting with a solution that seems desirable for one reason or another and then searching for problems to which the solution can be applied. The second section illustrates the practice of institutional diagnostics by comparing and contrasting the cases of climate change and biological diversity in order to illuminate differences in the sorts of governance systems needed in order to make progress in dealing with these problems. There is no presumption here that all it takes is careful analysis to succeed in finding ways to solve these problems. Failures in efforts to meet needs for governance are common at all levels of social organization at all times and in all places. Nevertheless, there are opportunities for improving our track record in building effective environmental governance systems. *Applied institutional analysis* can play a significant role in taking advantage of these opportunities.

Institutional Diagnostics

The link between the propositions that analysts produce and the solutions to specific problems that practitioners seek centers on diagnosis, or, in other words, the identification of key features of specific problems and the application of relevant propositions to guide the process of crafting governance systems to solve these problems case by case. In practice how does this process work? The way forward in this realm is to launch a series of diagnostic queries that those who have in-depth knowledge of the problem to be solved can answer and then to make use of the answers provided when thinking about the elements of the regime needed to solve it.[2] Does the issue involve a collective-action problem? Are the actors involved likely to experience incentives to cheat once they agree on the terms of a suitable regime? Is nonlinear and abrupt change likely in the issue area? Overcoming collective-action problems may require an effort to introduce regime elements based on the logic of appropriateness in order to supplement ideas derived exclusively from the logic of consequences.[3] Once put in place, solutions to some collective-action problems (e.g., those belonging to the category known as battle of the sexes) do not generate incentives to cheat, whereas solutions to others (e.g., those belonging to the category known as prisoner's dilemma) do generate powerful and persistent incentives to cheat.[4] Expending energy and political capital on the development of compliance mechanisms is essential in the latter case but not the former. What works in stable situations may prove highly ineffective in dealing with problems that are characterized by nonlinear and abrupt changes.[5]

Institutional diagnostics has much in common with other applied sciences, such as engineering and architecture. An engineer asked to design a bridge to be installed in a specific location will proceed by launching a range of queries pertaining to the biophysical features of the relevant site and the socioeconomic features of the relevant user group: How long a span is needed? What is the nature of the geology at either end? What volume of traffic will the bridge need to handle? Will this include rail traffic as well as road traffic? Is a certain clearance off the water required? What are the projections regarding growth in traffic in the future? Are there important budget constraints? All these factors must be considered when developing a suitable design. Similar considerations arise in the case of architecture: What are the expected uses of the building under consideration? Who are the expected users, and what are their needs? How many square feet are required for various uses? Are there zoning ordinances and building codes that need to be taken into account? What characteristics of the site are relevant? Are there features of the neighborhood that should be considered?

Are there projections about the future of the community that are relevant? Are there financial constraints that need to be respected? In both cases the basic message is the same. The design of a bridge or a building must take these factors into account in order to optimize the fit between the biophysical and socioeconomic settings and the solution selected.

Applied Institutional Analysis

Applied institutional analysis involves a similar process. We proceed by launching a suite of diagnostic queries: What is the nature of the problem? Who are the relevant actors? Is collective action a concern, or is the problem one of full-cost accounting to deal with unintended side effects? Does the group include a dominant actor or a hegemon? If not, are there a few actors who can come together as a leadership group? Are there broader constitutive arrangements or operative social practices in the relevant setting that will apply to any governance system created to deal with the specific problem? Is compliance likely to loom as a major concern in the administration of the regime? If so, what are the options for establishing effective compliance mechanisms? Does a central axis of conflict that divides the players into rival factions or coalitions dominate the overarching political setting? Or are there cross-cutting cleavages that dampen the effects of conflict relating to specific issues? These questions illustrate the sorts of diagnostic queries that come into focus in any exercise in applied institutional analysis. But many queries will be specific to individual situations, and gifted diagnosticians are those who have a talent for framing queries that elicit particularly important insights about specific situations.

Some analysts seek to array environmental problems along a spectrum on which those that are easy to solve lie at one end and those that are hard to solve are located at the other.[6] Many regard the problem of climate change, for instance, as a particularly hard problem to solve; they are apt to describe it as malign, or wicked, or even diabolical, concluding that this problem may overwhelm our capacity to come up with effective solutions.[7] I do not doubt that climate change presents a stiff challenge, but from the perspective of applied institutional analysis, this is not a particularly helpful way to approach the problem. We do not need to be told that this problem may prove insoluble when it comes to devising a governance system that is able to deal with it effectively. We do need to identify key features of the problem that must be taken into account in thinking about the attributes of the governance system needed to come to terms with it. Applied institutional analysis is not about ranking problems on some scale relating to how hard they may be to solve; rather, it is about devising regimes that fit the essential features of the problems at hand, thereby maximizing chances of success in problem solving.

Climate and Biodiversity

To make the idea of institutional diagnostics more concrete, I turn in this section to the problems of climate change and the loss of biological diversity, exploring similarities and differences between the two cases that are relevant in thinking about requirements for solving these problems. These cases loom large among the environmental challenges facing societies today. They are both highly complex issues that present challenges running all the way from the local to the global levels. Yet there are also differences between them that are illuminating when it comes to seeking insights about the nature of the regimes needed to produce solutions. The following account is by no means exhaustive. Any clever diagnostician will be able to come up with additional concerns that will generate helpful insights about the problems of climate change and the loss of biological diversity. But this discussion should help illuminate the nature of applied institutional analysis.

Problem Type

Climate change presents a systemic problem. The Earth's climate system is planetary in scope. Emissions of greenhouse gases (GHGs) occurring anywhere will add to overall concentrations of GHGs in the atmosphere; reductions in emissions anywhere will slow the rate of increase in concentrations in the atmosphere as a whole. Biodiversity, however, presents a cumulative problem.[8] By and large the loss of species in one ecosystem is not likely to have a direct impact on the status of species in other ecosystems, though adding up developments in many different ecosystems makes it possible to arrive at a kind of global box score with regard to the status of biodiversity. What is needed to address climate change is a global regime applicable to the behavior of all those who emit GHGs. Because the result will be a public good on a global scale, dealing with free-riders is almost certain to emerge as a major concern. What is needed to protect biodiversity, by contrast, is a collection of arrangements tailored to the circumstances prevailing in particularly important locations (e.g., the Amazon Basin, Madagascar) and focused in many cases on the challenge of controlling unintended side effects of actions designed to promote economic development.

Functional Scope

The effectiveness of efforts to address climate change is sensitive to what happens in related issue areas. The regime articulated in the UN Framework Convention on Climate Change (UNFCCC) constitutes the central thrust of efforts to deal with climate change. But the regime dealing with ozone-depleting substances set forth in the 1987 Montreal Protocol has done more to reduce emissions of GHGs than the climate regime, and efforts to address the climate impacts of carbon soot are likely to evolve outside the climate regime mainstream. Developments in other issue areas, such as adjustments to the global trade regime, are also likely to have far-reaching consequences for efforts to deal with climate change. In the case of the loss of biological diversity the core response is articulated in the Convention on Biological Diversity (CBD). But there are important linkages to a number of other arrangements, including regulations pertaining to commercial shipping that affect the spread of invasive species, the regime dealing with international trade in endangered species of wild fauna and flora, the provisions of the WTO allowing for exemptions to free-trade rules designed to address certain environmental concerns, and a wide range of domestic regimes dealing with land use and the regulation of freshwater. Although the two cases differ significantly in the nature of the most relevant functional linkages, it is clear that we need to focus in both cases on the development of effective regime complexes rather than thinking only about strengthening the UNFCCC or the CBD.[9]

Spatial Extent

Although the climate system is planetary in scope, emissions of GHGs are not distributed evenly around the planet. Between them the United States and China account for over 40 percent of the emissions of these gases. Adding Brazil, India, Russia, and the European Union brings us to two-thirds of the global emissions. This means that a coalition encompassing a relatively small number of players could take effective steps to curtail emissions of GHGs in contrast to the set of 190-plus countries that are active in meetings of the UNFCCC Conference of the Parties, where strong norms of consensus prevail. In the case of biodiversity the critical insight is that there is a relatively small number of "hot spots" that are critical from the point of view of species loss. The situation here differs dramatically from the case of climate change because forming a coalition among those countries where the hot spots are located is not essential. What is needed instead is a suite of measures on the part of key countries (e.g., Brazil, Indonesia, Madagascar), most likely with material support on the part of wealthy developed countries, to slow the loss of habitat and control the spread of invasive species on a case-by-case basis.

Driving Forces

Two great forces lie at the heart of climate change: the use of fossil fuels to generate energy for all sorts of industrial, commercial, and residential purposes, and deforestation to make way for agriculture or generate wood products for numerous uses. The use of fossil fuels is deeply embedded in advanced industrial societies; the need to find new land suitable for agriculture is a powerful force in a world of seven billion people and counting. Major drivers of bio-diversity loss include the loss of habitat and the spread of invasive species as well as the depletion of stocks of living resources through consumptive use and the eradication of species treated as pests. Climate change itself is a major force affecting the future of many species. To make progress in dealing with climate change, there is no substitute for transforming industrial economies in such a way as to reduce drastically their dependence on fossil fuels. This is the essential concern of those who call for a shift toward a "green economy."[10] In the case of biodiversity, by contrast, there is much to be said for strategies like creating large marine and terrestrial protected areas and corridors that allow migratory species to move from one segment of their range to others. One of the most significant things that could be done to slow the loss of biological diversity would be to address the problem of climate change effectively. Thus, the two problems are linked in an important way.

Actors

The actions of those operating all the way from the local to the global levels affect both climate change and the loss of biodiversity. In the case of biodiversity a striking feature of the problem is that actions affecting an area as small as a single hectare of land can drive some species (including many that have not been identified explicitly) to extinction. For its part climate change is driven by the decisions of individuals making choices about where to live and what sorts of transportation to use as well as the decisions of policy-makers operating at the national level and even at the international level, as in the case of the Conference of the Parties to the UNFCCC. Successful responses in both cases will depend on finding ways to influence a wide range of actors. This raises the question of the extent to which the logic of appropriateness as well as the logic of consequences influences key actors' behavior. Is there room, for example, to make a difference regarding the problem of biodiversity by cultivating what Aldo Leopold described as a "land ethic"?[11] Can we hope to reduce GHG emissions through measures that appeal to a discourse of environmental stewardship rather than relying exclusively on incentive mechanisms?[12] In both cases it is important to think about the relative merits of efforts to influence the behavior of large numbers of individuals directly rather than concentrating on the actions of a small number of policymakers. These are not either/or choices, but given the competition for scarce resources and the opportunity costs associated with selecting specific strategies, assumptions about actor behavior that guide choices of strategies for addressing climate change and biodiversity loss are likely to have far-reaching consequences for the success of the regimes we create.

Costs

Estimates of the costs of addressing problems like climate change and the loss of biological diversity along with the costs of doing nothing are important to the success of efforts to form effective regimes. In the case of the depletion of stratospheric ozone, for example, a report produced in the mid-1980s indicating that the costs arising from the long-term impacts of this phenomenon on human health would far outweigh the costs of finding substitutes for ozone-depleting substances played an important role in animating efforts to reach agreement on the terms of the 1987 Montreal Protocol.[13] A major complication regarding both climate and biodiversity is that efforts to estimate both the costs of action and those of inaction are subject to profound uncertainties. This is partly a consequence of the debate about appropriate discount rates to be used in thinking about future benefits and costs. But even more important are the uncertainties about what the true costs are likely to be and the lack of appropriate procedures for making meaningful cost estimates in the case of nonmarket goods and services. It is not surprising under the circumstances that interested parties differ dramatically in their conclusions about costs. Climate skeptics assert that the costs of reducing GHG emissions substantially would be prohibitive; those opposed to far-reaching measures to protect biological diversity question the contributions to social welfare to be derived from protecting species and emphasizing ecosystem services. Their opponents produce conclusions suggesting that there are affordable ways to solve the problem of climate change and that the consequences arising from the loss of biodiversity are profound.[14] It is apparent that these disagreements arise, in part, from differences in value systems in contrast to differences in propositions about factual matters relating to the consequences of climate change and the loss of biodiversity. The ensuing battles about both the costs of taking the steps needed to avoid serious climate change and biodiversity loss and the costs likely to arise from a policy of inaction are among the most important impediments to establishing effective regimes to deal with these problems.[15]

Distributive Concerns

The Earth's climate system is planetary in scope, and maintaining biological diversity is of interest to people everywhere. Yet clearly the impacts of climate change and the loss of biodiversity will not be uniform across the planet's human communities. Small island developing states and low-lying coastal areas are most at risk from the impacts of climate change. By contrast, some areas in the high latitudes could actually benefit from the early stages of climate change, though it is probably an illusion to suppose that any areas will benefit as the impacts of climate change become more severe. A disturbing feature of climate change is that there is likely to be a significant disconnect between those whose actions cause the problem and those most likely to be victimized by the impacts of the problem. The loss of biological diversity will impinge on the well-being of people everywhere and will be measured in terms of amenity values. But the consequent disruption of ecosystems will be especially harmful to those located where the disruptions occur. A particularly serious concern arises from the fact that urban dwellers and others who are somewhat sheltered from the direct effects of biodiversity loss are in a position to exert great influence on policy choices that will determine the trajectory of this problem. More generally a major challenge for governance arises whenever the costs associated with an environmental problem fall disproportionately on those whose actions are not major sources of the problem. Victims whose bargaining power is limited are especially likely to suffer.

Equity

This discussion raises questions about matters of equity or fairness arising in connection with problems like climate change and biodiversity loss. It is hard to see any normatively respectable justification for adopting a policy of grandfathering the allocation of emissions permits under the terms of a regime dedicated to reducing emissions of GHGs.[16] Considerations of fairness in this case would seem to require a policy taking as a point of departure the proposition that permits should be allocated among all the world's people on an equal per capita basis. Assuming that these permits would be transferable, such an arrangement could generate the revenue needed to fund serious adaptation measures in the developing world. In the case of biodiversity, issues of fairness come to the fore in thinking about the interests of local users of living resources, developers seeking to use land for purposes likely to prove harmful to species, and distant people who derive satisfaction or pleasure from the existence of polar bears, tigers, and pandas. There is no simple procedure for dealing with conflicts among these interests; efforts to use monetary compensation for damages arising from the loss of biodiversity cannot succeed in this case. From the perspective of those endeavoring to create successful environmental regimes, however, it is important to note that compliance with the terms of these arrangements is likely to be substantially higher among those who feel that the regimes are fundamentally fair or equitable in contrast to those who believe that their interests have been ignored or marginalized.

Compliance

As the preceding observation suggests, compliance with the terms of environmental regimes is not simply a matter of presenting actors with benefit-cost calculations that make compliance rational.[17]

What has become known as monitoring, reporting, and verification is important when pursuing compliance in every setting. There is no way to assess levels of compliance, much less to initiate actions designed to raise levels of compliance, in the absence of some capacity to track subjects' actions. The cases of climate change and the loss of biodiversity make it abundantly clear how hard it is to track the relevant behavior with any precision. Partly, this is a matter of the sheer number of actors involved. GHG emissions occur worldwide in conjunction with a wide range of activities. In part, it is a matter of tracking clandestine behavior on the part of those making a deliberate effort to circumvent the rules of environmental regimes. The challenges facing those responsible for monitoring international trade in animals and plants listed in Appendix 1 of the Convention on International Trade in Endangered Species of Wild Fauna and Flora (CITES) exemplify this issue dramatically.[18] What this means is that efforts to promote compliance with the provisions of environmental regimes must appeal to the logic of appropriateness as well as that of consequences.[19] This is one place where considerations of good governance enter the picture. In cases like climate change and biodiversity loss, where regimes' effectiveness requires compliance on an ongoing basis, there is much to be said for making a concerted effort to maximize transparency and accountability on the part of those responsible for administering regimes over time.

Adaptability

Regimes operating under the conditions of the Anthropocene (e.g., the arrangements founded on the provisions of the UNFCCC and the CBD) will need to be able to function effectively in turbulent times.[20] In some instances changes in biophysical or socioeconomic circumstances that are both nonlinear and abrupt will confront them. The current discussion in the scientific community about tipping elements in the Earth's climate system makes it clear that such changes are possible—even likely—in the case of climate change, though making predictions about developments like the disintegration of ice sheets or dramatic changes in thermohaline circulation is not easy.[21] Parallel challenges in the case of biodiversity are likely to focus on the analysis of complex ecosystems. But documenting processes leading to sharp shifts in the dynamics of ecosystems resulting from the loss of keystone species is not difficult.[22] The implications of these observations for governance are easy to identify but difficult to address effectively. Both the climate regime and the biodiversity regime need to be able to adapt quickly to changing circumstances, moving to respond agilely to new developments in a timely manner. This is not an impossible requirement. The pace at which the regime for protecting stratospheric ozone developed in the wake of new evidence regarding the scope and consequences of the thinning of the ozone layer is striking.[23] Nonetheless, this will be a major challenge in cases like climate change and the loss of biological diversity, where efforts to adjust the relevant regimes are likely to involve conference diplomacy in which there is a need to satisfy large numbers of actors with diverse interests. In the near future this will certainly lead to growing pressures to move important discussions about the development of these regimes to smaller venues, such as the meetings of the Group of Twenty Finance Ministers and Central Bank Governors (the G-20).

Conclusion

Where does this leave us with respect to applied institutional analysis, and what are the next steps in this domain? Crafting effective regimes to deal with environmental problems will require a consideration of the distinctive features of individual cases. Yet some insights emerge from the discussion of the problems of climate change and biodiversity loss that are sure to have wider application. Matching governance systems to problems is more important than rating problems in terms of some criterion of hardness. Regime complexes are likely to be the order of the day in addressing multidimensional problems, especially under the conditions characteristic of the Anthropocene. An emphasis on understanding the dynamics of multilevel governance and finding ways to take advantage of interactions across levels of social organization so as to produce synergy in the realm of environmental governance will be critical. In cases in which steering or guiding behavior on an ongoing basis is necessary, addressing concerns about equity or fairness and paying attention to matters like transparency and accountability in the administration of environmental regimes are important. Increasingly, success in the creation and administration of these regimes will require the cultivation of coalitions among the public sector, the private sector, and civil society. There is much to be said for paying attention to reforming key elements of the deep structure that provides the foundation for constructing regimes that address problems like climate change and the loss of biological diversity. Developing a capacity to adapt to nonlinear and sometimes abrupt changes in biophysical and socioeconomic settings is essential.

We need to reckon with the fact that both the creation and the administration of governance systems are profoundly political processes.[24] These processes are driven by actors seeking to advance their own interests rather than those dedicated to some notion of the public interest or the common good. In the absence of a dominant actor capable of imposing order or a high level of consensus around matters of deep structure, institutional bargaining will be fraught with competing visions about the way forward in creating and adjusting environmental regimes. Often this will generate a condition of deadlock in which making progress relative to the status quo will be difficult. Nonetheless, to infer from this that there is no prospect of making progress in addressing the major environmental problems of our era would be a mistake. Not only do fundamental visions of human-environment relations shift on a decadal time scale, but windows of opportunity also emerge from time to time in which sharp shifts in governance systems become feasible. Like biophysical systems, political systems experience tipping points leading to nonlinear and occasionally abrupt changes. Such occurrences are difficult to anticipate. Even those who are attuned to such matters may not recognize them right away. Under the circumstances there is much to be said not only for keeping a sharp eye out for signs that we are approaching political tipping points but also for thinking in advance about the options for substantial changes in environmental regimes that may become feasible in the wake of such tipping points. Success in creating effective environmental regimes to deal with the problems of the Anthropocene will depend on developing a clear sense of alternatives that are preferable to the status quo coupled with an ability to act decisively when windows of opportunity arise.

In the end it is essential to remember that environmental governance is a matter of guiding or steering human actions in such a way as to avoid vicious cycles like the race to catch the last fish or the competition to attract investors with promises of lax environmental standards and, instead, to encourage virtuous cycles like the competition to develop climate-friendly and affordable energy systems. There is no need to despair about the prospects for succeeding in this effort, even with regard to large-scale problems like climate change and the loss of biodiversity. But the effort to address such problems will require both a major push to enlist the social sciences in addressing the challenges of environmental governance and a serious commitment to improving the dialogue between science and policy in this realm. Nothing could be more important than rising to this challenge—the success of the human enterprise in the Anthropocene depends on it.

NOTES

Introduction: Governing Human-Environment Relations

1. On human domination of the Earth system, see Peter Vitousek, Harold Mooney, Jane Lubchenco, and Jerry Melillo, "Human Domination of the Earth's Ecosystems," *Science* 277 (1997): 494–99.

2. This challenge is spelled out in Will Steffen, Paul J. Crutzen, and John R. McNeill, "The Anthropocene: Are Humans Overwhelming the Great Forces of Nature?" *Ambio* 36 (2007): 614–21.

3. For an overview of governance as a social function, see Oran R. Young, "Governance for Sustainable Development in a World of Rising Interdependencies," in Magali A. Delmas and Oran R. Young, eds., *Governance for the Environment: New Perspectives,* 12–40 (Cambridge: Cambridge University Press, 2009).

4. This observation has stimulated a growing interest in governance without government. See James N. Rosenau and Ernst-Otto Czempiel, eds., *Governance Without Government: Order and Change in World Politics* (Cambridge: Cambridge University Press, 1992).

5. Elinor Ostrom et al., eds., *The Drama of the Commons* (Washington, DC: National Academies Press, 2002).

6. See Magali A. Delmas and Oran R. Young, eds., *Governance for the Environment: New Perspectives* (Cambridge: Cambridge University Press, 2009).

7. Oran R. Young, et al., *Institutional Dimensions of Global Environment Change (IDGEC) Science Plan* (Bonn: IHDP Report Nos. 9, 16, 1999/2005).

8. For a classic account of international society see Hedley Bull, *The Anarchical Society: A Study of Order in World Politics* (New York: Columbia University Press, 1977).

9. Bruce M. S. Campbell and Ricardo Godoy, "Commonfield Agriculture: The Andes and Medieval England Compared," in Daniel W. Bromley, ed., *Making the Commons Work: Theory, Practice, and Policy,* 99–127 (San Francisco: ICS Press, 1992).

10. On UNCLOS see Alex G. Oude Elferink, ed., *Stability and Change in the Law of the Sea: The Role of the LOS Convention* (Leiden: Martinus Nijhoff Publishers, 2005).

11. Paul A. Berkman, Michael A. Lang, David W. H. Walton, and Oran R. Young, eds., *Science Diplomacy: Antarctica, Science, and the Governance of International Spaces* (Washington, DC: Smithsonian Institution Scholarly Press, 2011).

12. For a seminal account see Thomas C. Schelling, *The Strategy of Conflict* (Cambridge, MA: Harvard University Press, 1960).

13. See Samuel P. Hays, *Conservation and the Gospel of Efficiency* (New York: Atheneum, 1975).

14. Oran R. Young, "Regime Dynamics: The Rise and Fall of International Regimes," *International Organization* 36 (1982): 277–97.

15. Oran R. Young, *Institutional Dynamics: Emergent Patterns in International Environmental Governance* (Cambridge, MA: MIT Press, 2010).

16. Oran R. Young, *Resource Regimes: Natural Resources and Social Institutions* (Berkeley: University of California Press, 1982).

17. Schelling, *The Strategy of Conflict*; and Russell Hardin, *Collective Action* (Baltimore, MD: Johns Hopkins University Press, 1982).

18. Garrett Hardin, "The Tragedy of the Commons," *Science* 162 (1968), 1243–48; and Mancur Olson Jr., *The Logic of Collective Action* (Cambridge, MA: Harvard University Press, 1965).

19. J. H. Dales, *Pollution, Property, and Prices: An Essay in Policy-Making and Economics* (Toronto: University of Toronto Press, 1968); and Daniel H. Cole, *Pollution and Property: Comparing Ownership Institutions for Environmental Protection* (Cambridge: Cambridge University Press, 2002).

20. Leigh Raymond, *Private Rights and Public Resources: Equity and Property Allocation in Market-Based Environmental Policy* (Washington, DC: Resources for the Future, 2003).

21. Henrik Enderlein, Sonja Wälti, and Michael Zürn, eds., *Handbook on Multi-level Governance* (Cheltenham, UK: Edward Elgar, 2010).

22. Arild Underdal, "Determining the Causal Significance of Institutions: Accomplishments and Challenges," in Oran R. Young, Leslie A. King, and Heike Schroeder, eds., *Institutions and Environmental Change,* 49–78 (Cambridge, MA: MIT Press, 2008).

23. Oran R. Young, "The Effectiveness of International Environmental Regimes: Existing Knowledge, Cutting-edge Themes, and Research Strategies," *Proceedings of the National Academy of Sciences* 108, no. 50 (December 13, 2011): 19853–60.

24. Ronald B. Mitchell, "Evaluating the Performance of Environmental Institutions: What to Evaluate and How to Evaluate It?" in Young, King, and Schroeder, eds., *Institutions and Environmental Change,* 79–114.

25. For a range of perspectives on the idea of good governance see Durwood Zaelke et al., eds., *Making Law Work: Environmental Compliance and Sustainable Development,* 2 vols. (London: Cameron, May 2005).

26. See the essays in "Going Beyond Panaceas," A Special Feature of the *Proceedings of the National Academy of Sciences* 104, no. 39 (September 25, 2007).

27. Victor Galaz et al., "The Problem of Fit Among Biophysical Systems, Environmental and Resource Regimes, and Broader Governance Systems: Insights and Emerging Issues," in Young, King, and Schroeder, eds., *Institutions and Environmental Change,* 147–86.

28. Oran R. Young, *The Institutional Dimensions of Environmental Change: Fit, Interplay, and Scale* (Cambridge, MA: MIT Press, 2002); Elinor Ostrom, "A Diagnostic Approach for Going Beyond Panaceas," *Proceedings of the National Academy of Sciences* 104 (September 25, 2007): 15181–87; Oran R. Young, "Building Regimes for Socioecological Systems: Institutional Diagnostics," in Young, King, and Schroeder, eds., *Institutions and Environmental Change,* 115–55.

29. See Thomas Dietz, Elinor Ostrom, and Paul C. Stern, "The Struggle to Govern the Commons," *Science* 302 (2003): 1907–12; and Oran R. Young, "Why Is There No Unified Theory of Environmental Governance?" in Peter Dauvergne, ed., *Handbook of Global Environmental Politics,* 170–84 (Cheltenham, UK: Edward Elgar Publishing, 2005).

30. See the essays in Oran R. Young, ed., *Global Governance: Drawing Insights from the Environmental Experience* (Cambridge, MA: MIT Press, 1997).

31. Oran R Young., "Navigating the Sustainability Transition," in Eric Brousseau et al., eds., *Global Environmental Commons: Analytical*

and Political Challenges in Building Governance Mechanisms (Oxford: Oxford University Press, forthcoming).

Chapter One Natural Resources

1. For a general account framed in terms of the idea of micromotives and macrobehavior see Thomas C. Schelling, *Micromotives and Macrobehavior* (New York: W. W. Norton, 1977).

2. Russell Hardin, *Collective Action* (Baltimore, MD: Johns Hopkins University Press, 1982).

3. H. Scott Gordon, "The Economic Theory of a Common Property Resource: The Fishery," *Journal of Political Economy* 62 (1954): 124–42; Anthony Scott, "The Fishery: The Objectives of Sole Ownership," *Journal of Political Economy* 63 (1955): 116–24; Garrett Hardin, "The Tragedy of the Commons," *Science* 162 (1968): 1243–48.

4. Oran R. Young, "Rights, Rules, and Common Pools: Solving Problems Arising in Human-Environment Relations," *Natural Resources Journal* 47 (2007): 1–16.

5. See Marshal Sahlins, *Stone Age Economics* (Chicago: Aldine, 1972) for an influential account of the idea of the "original affluent society."

6. For a review see Arun Agrawal, "Common Resources and Institutional Sustainability," in Elinor Ostrom et al., eds., *The Drama of the Commons,* 41–85 (Washington, DC: National Academies Press, 2002).

7. John A. Baden and Douglas Noonan, eds., *Managing the Commons* (Bloomington: Indiana University Press, 1998).

8. Elinor Ostrom, *Governing the Commons: The Evolution of Institutions for Collective Action* (Cambridge: Cambridge University Press, 1990).

9. Terry L. Anderson and Donald R. Leal, *Free Market Environmentalism,* rev. ed. (San Francisco: Pacific Research Institute, 2001).

10. Daniel Fife, "Killing to Goose," *Environment* 13, no. 3 (1971): 20, 27.

11. Christopher McGrory Klyza, *Who Controls Public Lands? Mining, Forestry, and Grazing Policies, 1870–1990* (Chapel Hill: University of North Carolina Press, 1996).

12. Gail Osherenko, "New Discourses on Ocean Rights: Understanding Property Rights, the Public Trust, and Ocean Governance," *Journal of Environmental Law and Litigation* 21 (2007): 105–67.

13. Leigh Raymond, *Private Rights in Public Resources: Allocation in Market-Based Environmental Policy* (Washington, DC: RFF Press, 2003).

14. For a trenchant case study dealing with limited-entry fisheries in Iceland see Niels Einarsson, *Culture, Conflict and Crisis in Icelandic Fisheries: An Anthropological Study of People, Policy and Marine Resources in the North Atlantic Arctic* (Uppsala, Sweden: University of Uppsala, 2011).

15. The value of commodities derives from consumptive use. The enjoyment of amenities, by contrast, does not require consumptive use. Thus, many can enjoy an amenity without detracting from the enjoyment of others. See John V. Krutilla and Anthony C. Fisher, *The Economics of Natural Environments: Studies in the Valuation of Commodity and Amenity Resources* (Baltimore, MD: Johns Hopkins University Press, 1975).

16. Mancur Olson Jr., *The Logic of Collective Acton* (Cambridge, MA: Harvard University Press, 1965).

17. Milton M. R. Freeman and Urs P. Kreuter, eds., *Elephants and Whales: Resources for Whom?* (Basel: Gordon and Breach, 1995).

18. Olson, *The Logic of Collective Acton*.

19. Scott Barrett, *Why Cooperate? The Incentive to Supply Global Public Goods* (New York: Oxford University Press, 2007).

20. On the role of hegemons, with particular reference to cooperation in large-scale societies, see Duncan Snidal, "The Limits of Hegemonic Stability Theory," *International Organization* 39 (1985): 579–614.

21. Olson, *The Logic of Collective Acton*.

22. Schelling, *Micromotives and Macrobehavior*.

23. On institutional bargaining see Oran R. Young, "The Politics of International Regime Formation: Managing Natural Resources and the Environment," *International Organization* 43 (1989): 349–75.

24. The idea of a "k group" is developed in Schelling, *Micromotives and Macrobehavior*, ch. 7.

25. On the distinction between compliance and enforcement see Oran R. Young, *Compliance and Public Authority: A Theory with International Applications* (Baltimore, MD: Johns Hopkins University Press, 1979).

26. The distinction between the logic of appropriateness and the logic of consequences is a matter of the extent to which the behavior of actors is influenced by considerations other than utilitarian and self-interested calculations. See James G. March and Johan P. Olsen, *Rediscovering Institutions: The Organizational Basis of Politics* (New York: The Free Press, 1989); and H. L. A. Hart, *The Concept of Law* (Oxford: Oxford University Press, 1961).

27. For a discussion of regimes as public goods see Oran R. Young, *International Governance: Protecting the Environment in a Stateless Society* (Ithaca, NY: Cornell University Press, 1994).

Chapter Two Environmental Protection

1. On the development of the nuisance doctrine and its application to contemporary environmental issues see William H. Rodgers Jr., *Handbook on Environmental Law* (St. Paul, MN: West Publishing Company, 1977), ch. 2.

2. For background on the idea of regulatory takings see Joseph L. Sax, "Takings, Private Property and Public Rights," *Yale Law Journal* 81 (1971): 149 et seq.; and Bruce Ackerman, *Private Property and the Constitution* (New Haven, CT: Yale University Press, 1972).

3. For an illuminating general discussion of rules see John Rawls, "Two Concepts of Rules," *Philosophical Review* 64 (1955): 3–32.

4. A seminal account of spontaneous or self-generating rules appears in Friedrich A. Hayek, *Law, Legislation, and Liberty,* vol. 1 of *Rules and Order* (Chicago: University of Chicago Press, 1973).

5. Robert C. Ellickson, *Order Without Law: How Neighbors Settle Disputes* (Cambridge, MA: Harvard University Press, 1991). A particularly interesting feature of the narrative that Ellickson presents is that the informal rules in this case arose in a setting in which more formal rules pertaining to the problem already existed.

6. For a prominent account of regulatory measures see Malcolm K. Sparrow, *The Regulatory Craft: Controlling Risks, Solving Problems, and Managing Compliance* (Washington, DC: Brookings Institution, 2000).

7. For an accessible introduction see Allan V. Kneese and Charles V. Shultze, *Pollution, Prices and Public Policy* (Washington, DC: Brookings Institution, 1975).

8. To see how these ideas play out in practice see J. H. Dales, *Pollution, Property and Prices: An Essay in Policy-Making and Economics* (Toronto: University of Toronto Press, 1968); and Daniel H. Cole, *Pollution and Property: Comparing Ownership Institutions for Environmental Protection* (Cambridge: Cambridge University Press, 2002).

9. Needless to say, those who think in terms of cost functions will be motivated to use as much as possible of a factor of production that is free.

10. Joseph E. Aldy and Robert N. Stavins, eds., *Architectures for Agreement: Addressing Climate Change in the Post-Kyoto World* (Cambridge: Cambridge University Press, 2007).

11. A. P. Kinzig et al., "Paying for Ecosystem Services—Promise and Peril," *Science* 334 (November 4, 2011): 603–4.

12. For a range of perspectives on this theme see Neil K. Komesar, *Law's Limits: Rule of Law and the Supply and Demand of Rights* (Cambridge: Cambridge University Press, 2001) and Durwood Zaelke et al., eds., *Making Law Work: Environmental Compliance and Sustainable Development,* 2 vols. (London: Cameron May, 2005).

13. Magala A. Delmas and Oran R. Young eds., *Governance for the Environment: New Perspectives* (Cambridge: Cambridge University Press, 2009).

14. Neil Gunningham and Darren Sinclair, *Leaders and Laggards: Next-Generation Environmental Regulation* (Sheffield, UK: Greenleaf Publishing, 2002).

15. Ronald H. Coase, "The Problem of Social Cost," *Journal of Law and Economics* 3 (1960): 1–44.

16. The validity of this conclusion depends on the assumption that there are no transaction costs or, in any case, that such costs do not impede interactions between the relevant actors. In cases in which those harmed by environmental side effects constitute a large and widely dispersed group, this assumption is particularly unrealistic.

17. Conflicts regarding such matters are particularly intense in the context of zoning. For an overview see "Zoning in the United States," Wikipedia, http://en.wikipedia.org/wiki/Zoning_in_the_United_States.

18. For a seminal work on liability rules relevant in this context see Guido Calabresi and Douglas Melamed, "Property Rules, Liability Rules, and Inalienability: One View of the Cathedral," *Harvard Law Review* 85 (1972): 1089–1128.

19. Leigh Raymond, *Property Rights in Public Resources: Equity and Property Allocation in Market-Based Environmental Policy* (Washington, DC: Resources for the Future, 2003).

20. For a discussion of these issues in the context of climate change see Oran R. Young, "Does Justice Matter in International Environmental Governance? Toward a Fair Deal on Climate," paper delivered at the Beijing Forum, November 2010. Various perspectives on climate ethics are included in Stephen Gardiner, Simon Caney, Dale Jamieson, and Henry Shue, eds., *Climate Ethics: Essential Readings* (Oxford: Oxford University Press, 2010).

21. For a prominent analysis of these concerns see Robert D. Bullard, *Dumping in Dixie: Race, Class, and Environmental Quality,* 3rd ed. (Boulder, CO: Westview Press, 2000).

22. See Zaelke et al., *Making Law Work*.

23. For an introduction to the phenomenon of iron triangles see Thomas A. Birkland, *An Introduction to the Policy Process: Theories, Concepts, and Models of Public Policy Making*, 2nd ed. (Armonk, NY: M. E. Sharpe, 2005), ch. 3.

24. For a well-informed account of climate politics see Eric Pooley, *The Climate War: True Believers, Power Brokers, and the Fight to Save the Earth* (New York: Hyperion, 2010).

25. The concept of institutional arthritis is developed in Mancur Olson Jr., *The Rise and Decline of Nations: Economic Growth, Stagflation, and Social Rigidities* (New Haven, CT: Yale University Press, 1982).

26. See Charles Wolf, *Markets or Governments: Choosing Between Imperfect Alternatives* (Cambridge, MA: MIT Press, 1988).

27. These three factors are the familiar variables in the formula I = PAT. See, inter alia, Paul Ehrlich and John Holdren, "Impact of Population Growth," *Science* 171 (1971): 1212–17.

28. James C. Hansen, *Storms of My Grandchildren: The Truth About the Coming Climate Catastrophe and Our Last Chance to Save Humanity* (New York: Bloomsbury USA, 2009).

Chapter Three Ecosystem Services

1. For a general and highly accessible introduction to thinking in systems see Donella H. Meadows, *Thinking in Systems: A Primer* (White River Junction, VT: Chelsea Green, 2008).

2. But we know now that hunter-gatherers living some ten to twenty thousand years BP played an important role in driving some megafauna to extinction.

3. Peter M. Vitousek, Harold Mooney, Jane Lubchenko, and Jerry Melillo, "Human Domination of Earth's Ecosystems," *Science* 277 (1997): 494–99.

4. Gretchen Daily, "Introduction," in G. C. Daily, ed., *Nature's Services: Societal Dependence on Natural Ecosystems*, 3 (Washington, DC: Island Press, 1997).

5. Robert Costanza et al., "The Value of the World's Ecosystem Services and Natural Capital," *Nature* 387 (1997): 253.

6. Millennium Ecosystem Assessment (MEA), *Ecosystems and Human Well-Being: Summary for Decision Makers* (Washington, DC: Island Press, 2005).

7. For a general discussion of forest management see Marion Clawson, *Forests for Whom and for What?* (Baltimore, MD: Johns Hopkins University Press, 1975).

8. MEA, *Ecosystems and Human Well-Being*.

9. A. P. Kinzig et al., "Paying for Ecosystem Services—Promise and Peril," *Science* 334 (November 4, 2011): 603–4.

10. For an overview of methods for valuing ecosystem services see Millennium Ecosystem Assessment (MEA), *Current State and Trends* (Washington, DC: Island Press, 2005), ch. 2.

11. Costanza et al., "The Value of the World's Ecosystem Services and Natural Capital," 253.

12. Ibid.

13. For an influential discussion of the idea of rights as trumps see Ronald Dworkin, *Taking Rights Seriously* (Cambridge, MA: Harvard University Press, 1978).

14. On principles of valuation that are nonanthropogenic in nature see Bill Devall and George Sessions, *Deep Ecology: Living as if Nature Mattered* (Salt Lake City, UT: Peregrine Smith, 1985).

15. For a discussion of principles of stewardship see F. Stuart Chapin, III, Gary Kofinas, and Carl Folke, eds., *Principles of Ecosystem Stewardship: Resilience-Based Natural Resource Management in a Changing World* (New York: Springer, 2009).

16. On the idea of roving bandits see Mancur Olson Jr., *Power and Prosperity* (New York: Basic Books, 2000) and F. Berkes et al., "Globalization, Roving Bandits, and Marine Resources," *Science* 311 (2006): 1557–58.

17. Under these conditions the happy combination often referred to as doing good while doing well is unlikely to occur.

18. For examples see John V. Krutilla and Anthony C. Fisher, *The Economics of Natural Environments: Studies in the Valuation of Commodity and Amenity Resources* (Baltimore, MD: Johns Hopkins University Press, 1975).

19. For a variety of perspectives on socioecological systems (SESs) see Lance H. Gunderson and C. S. Holling, eds., *Panarchy: Understanding Transformation in Human and Natural Systems* (Washington, DC: Island Press, 2002).

20. For examples pertaining to forests see Emilo Moran and Elinor Ostrom, eds., *Seeing the Forests and the Trees: Human-Environment Interactions in Forest Ecosystems* (Cambridge, MA: MIT Press, 2005).

21. Aldo Leopold, "The Land Ethic," in Aldo Leopold, *A Sand County Almanac with Essays on Conservation from Round River* (New York: Ballantine Books, 1970), 262.

22. A number of state governments have what are generally known as "current use" tax programs, the purpose of which is to encourage landowners to maintain land in an undeveloped state by giving them tax breaks for doing so.

23. On the bases of the public trust doctrine see Joseph L. Sax, "The Public Trust Doctrine in Natural Resources Law: Effective Judicial Intervention," *Michigan Law Review* 68 (1970): 473–566.

24. For a variety of perspectives on policies pertaining to public lands see Lynton Keith Caldwell and Kristin Shrader-Frechette, *Policy for Land: Law and Ethics* (Lanham, MD: Rowman and Littlefield, 1993).

25. On the origins of the idea of wilderness see Roderick F. Nash, *Wilderness and the American Mind* (New Haven, CT: Yale University Press, 1967).

26. On the assertion of public authority over airsheds in American law see Gary Bryner, *Blue Skies, Green Politics: The Clean Air Act of 1990* (Washington, DC: CQ Press, 1993).

27. On the origins and principles of Earth System Science see Will Steffen et al., *Global Change and the Earth System: A Planet Under Pressure* (Berlin: Springer Verlag, 2004).

Chapter Four   Horizontal Interplay

1. On the resultant functional fragmentation see Larry Crowder et al., "Resolving Mismatches in U.S. Ocean Governance," *Science* 313 (2006): 617–18.

2. On the prospect that institutional interplay can lead to synergy rather than conflict see Sebastian Oberthür and Thomas Gehring, eds., *Institutional Interaction in Global Environmental Governance: Synergy and Conflict Among International and EU Policies* (Cambridge, MA: MIT Press, 2006).

3. An early but influential set of distinctions among types of interplay appears in Oran R. Young et al., *Institutional Dimensions of Global Environmental Change (IDGEC) Science Plan*, Report no. 9 (Bonn, Germany: IHDP, 1999).

4. On the concern that regime congestion can lead to increased interference see Edith Brown Weiss, "International Environmental Issues and

the Emergence of a New World Order," *Georgetown Law Journal* 81 (1993): 675–710.

5. See Guus J. M. Velders et al., "The Importance of the Montreal Protocol in Protecting Climate," *Proceedings of the National Academy of Sciences* 104 (2007): 4814–19.

6. See Young et al., *Institutional Dimensions of Global Environmental Change (IDGEC) Science Plan;* and Oran R. Young, *The Institutional Dimensions of Environmental Change: Fit, Interplay, and Scale* (Cambridge, MA: MIT Press, 2002).

7. M. Molina, D. Zaelke, K. H. Sarma, S. O. Andersen, V. Ramanathan, and D. Kaniaru, "Reducing Abrupt Climate Change Risk Using the Montreal Protocol and Other Regulatory Actions to Complement Cuts in CO_2 Emissions," *Proceedings of the National Academy of Sciences* 106 (2009): 20616–21.

8. On the case of biosafety see O. R. Young, W. B. Chambers, J. A. Kim, and C. ten Have, eds., *Institutional Interplay: Biosafety and Trade* (Tokyo: UN University Press, 2008); on the case of ocean governance see Karen McLeod and Heather Leslie, eds., *Ecosystem-Based Management for the Oceans* (Washington, DC: Island Press, 2009).

9. Oran R. Young, "Institutional Linkages in International Society: Polar Perspectives," *Global Governance* 2 (1996): 1–24.

10. Oberthür and Gehring, eds., *Institutional Interaction in Global Environmental Governance.*

11. For an account exploring the deep structure underpinning federal land law in the United States see Christopher McGrory Klyza, *Who Controls Public Lands? Mining, Forestry, and Grazing Policies, 1870–1990* (Chapel Hill: University of North Carolina Press, 1996).

12. Kal Rautiala and David G. Victor, "The Regime Complex for Plant Genetic Resources," *International Organization* 55 (2004): 277–309; and Robert O. Keohane and David G. Victor, "The Regime Complex for Climate Change," *Perspectives on Politics* 9 (2011): 7–23.

13. Young, *The Institutional Dimensions of Environmental Change,* ch. 5.

14. Christopher C. Joyner, *Governing the Frozen South: The Antarctic Regime and Environmental Protection* (Columbia: University of South Carolina Press, 1998).

15. For an overview of federal land law see George C. Coggins, Charles F. Wilkinson, John D. Leshy, and Robert L. Fischman, *Federal Public Land and Resources Law,* 6th ed. (St. Paul, MN: West Publishing Co., 2007).

16. See White House Council on Environmental Quality, *Final Recommendations of the Interagency Ocean Policy Task Force*, July 19, 2010, www.whitehouse.gov.

17. Robert L. Friedheim, *Negotiating the New Ocean Regime* (Columbia: University of South Carolina Press, 1993).

18. Young et al., *Institutional Interplay*.

19. McLeod and Leslie, *Ecosystem-Based Management for the Oceans*.

20. In August 2009 the US federal government imposed a moratorium on commercial fishing in the Beaufort Sea, citing the need to improve understanding of the impacts of climate change on this large marine ecosystem. No such moratorium has been imposed on offshore oil and gas development in the region.

21. See the essays in Richard H. Steinberg, ed., *The Greening of Trade Law: International Trade Organizations and Environmental Issues* (Lanham, MD.: Rowman and Littlefield, 2002).

22. On the future of UNEP see Frank Biermann and Stefan Bauer, eds., *A World Environment Organization: Solution or Threat for Effective International Environmental Governance?* (Aldershot, UK: Ashgate, 2005). The case of ocean governance is discussed in Oran R. Young et al., "Solving the Crisis in Ocean Governance: Place-Based Management of Marine Ecosystems," *Environment* 49 (May 2007): 20–32.

23. Oran R. Young, "The Architecture of Global Environmental Governance: Bringing Science to Bear on Policy," *Global Environmental Politics* 8 (2008): 14–32.

24. Bruce M. S. Campbell and Ricardo A. Godoy, "Commonfield Agriculture: The Andes and Medieval England Compared," in Daniel W. Bromley, ed., *Making the Commons Work: Theory, Practice, and Policy,* 99–127 (San Francisco: ICS Press, 1992).

25. On the legacy of the Trail Smelter case see Rebecca M. Bratspies and Russell A. Miller, eds., *Transboundary Harm in International Law: Lessons from the Trail Smelter Arbitration* (Cambridge: Cambridge University Press, 2006).

26. See Anthony Aust, *Modern Treaty Law and Practice* (Cambridge: Cambridge University Press, 2000), esp. ch. 12.

27. The US federal government often uses interagency committees to deal with issues of this sort. But the track record of such committees in achieving effective coordination is poor.

28. Jon Day, "Zoning: Lessons from the Great Barrier Marine Park," *Ocean and Coastal Management* 45 (2002): 139–56.

29. Young et al., "Solving the Crisis in Ocean Governance."

30. Amandine Orsini, Jean-Frederic Morin, and Oran R. Young, "Regime Complexes: A Buzz, a Boom, or a Boost for Global Governance?" *Global Governance,* forthcoming.

31. Sebastian Oberthür and Olav Schram Stokke, eds., *Institutional Interaction and Global Environmental Change* (Cambridge, MA: MIT Press, 2011).

Chapter Five Vertical Interplay

1. See Fikret Berkes, "Cross-Scale Institutional Linkages: Perspectives from the Bottom Up," in Elinor Ostrom et al., eds., *The Drama of the Commons,* 293–321 (Washington, DC: National Academy Press, 2002); and Oran R. Young, "Institutional Interplay: The Environmental Consequences of Cross-Scale Interactions," in Ostrom et al., eds., *The Drama of the Commons,* 263–91.

2. For a general treatment of multilevel governance see Henrik Enderlein, Sonja Wälti, and Michael Zürn, eds., *Handbook on Multi-Level Governance* (Cheltenham, UK: Edward Elgar, 2010).

3. See Pauline Maier, *Ratification: The People Debate the Constitution* (New York: Simon and Shuster, 2010).

4. For a more general account of federalism and subsidiarity see Steven G. Calabresi and Lucy D. Pickford, "Federalism and Subsidiarity: Perspectives from Law," paper presented at the annual meeting of the American Society for Political and Legal Philosophy, 2011.

5. For a history of confederation in Canada see "Canadian Confederation," Wikipedia, http://en.wikipedia.org/wiki/Canadian_Confederation.

6. The allocation of authority between the states and the federal government has been a contentious issue throughout the history of the United States. On the debates about this issue in conjunction with the framing and ratification of the Constitution and the crafting of the Bill of Rights, see Maier, *Ratification.*

7. For a good overview see James Salzman and Barton H. Thompson Jr., *Environmental Law and Policy,* 3rd ed. (New York: Foundation Press, 2010).

8. Barry G. Rabe, "Beyond Kyoto: Climate Change Policy in Multilevel Governance Systems," *Governance* 20 (2007): 423–44.

9. The most prominent example is the UN initiative on Reducing Emissions from Deforestation and Forest Degradation (REDD+), developed under the auspices of the UN Framework Convention on Climate Change.

10. Michael J. Bean and Melanie J. Rowland, *The Evolution of National Wildlife Law*, 3rd ed. (Westport, CT: Praeger, 1997).

11. Simon Lyster, *International Wildlife Law: An Analysis of International Treaties Concerned with the Conservation of Wildlife* (Cambridge: Cambridge University Press, 1993).

12. See Harriet Bulkeley and Michele M. Betsill, *Cities and Climate Change: Urban Sustainability and Global Environmental Governance* (London: Routledge, 2003).

13. For a variety of perspectives on the authority of the United Nations and its limitations see Thomas G. Weiss and Sam Daws, eds., *The Oxford Handbook on the United Nations* (Oxford: Oxford University Press, 2007).

14. See, for example, Benjamin Cashore, Graeme Auld, and Deanna Newsome, *Governing Through Markets: Forest Certification and the Emergence of Non-State Authority* (New Haven, CT: Yale University Press, 2004).

15. See Don Munton, Marvin Soroos, Elena Nikitina, and Marc Levy, "Acid Rain in Europe and North America," in Oran R. Young, ed., *The Effectiveness of International Environmental Regimes*, 155–247 (Cambridge, MA: MIT Press, 1999).

16. The Copenhagen Accord is a policy statement issued at the conclusion of the 15th Conference of the Parties to the UN Framework Convention of Climate Change. The text is available at www.unfccc.int.

17. See Barry Rabe, *Statehouse and Greenhouse: The Emerging Politics of American Climate Change Policy* (Washington, DC: Brookings Institution, 2004).

18. The key Supreme Court decision is *Massachusetts v. EPA*, 127 S. Ct. at 1438 (2007).

19. See the Supreme Court decision in *Connecticut v. AEPC*, 564 S. Ct. slip opinion (2011).

20. See the Supreme Court decision in *Environmental Defense v. Duke Energy*, 549 S. Ct. slip opinion (2007).

21. For a general discussion of subsidiarity see Calabresi and Bickford, "Federalism and Subsidiarity."

22. See Derek Armitage, Fikret Berkes, and Nancy Doubleday, *Adaptive Co-Management: Collaboration, Learning, and Multilevel Governance* (Vancouver: University of British Columbia Press, 2007).

23. The comanagement arrangement for the Porcupine Caribou Herd is discussed in ibid.

24. An interesting feature of this case was the Obama Administration's opposition to the states' position on the grounds that federal law in the form of the Clean Air Act Amendments of 1990 preempts state action in this realm.

25. In an ongoing case known as *Texas v. EPA*, the state argues that federal regulations in this area run counter to state law and are therefore unenforceable within its jurisdiction.

26. For a general account of NEPA see Lynton K. Caldwell, *The National Environmental Policy Act: An Agenda for the Future* (Bloomington: Indiana University Press, 1999).

27. On the consequences of recent trends toward decentralizing public authority in some parts of the world see Krister Andersson, Gustavo Gordillo de Anda, and Frank van Laerhoven, *Local Government and Rural Development: Comparing Lessons from Brazil, Chile, Mexico, and Peru* (Tucson: University of Arizona Press, 2009).

Chapter Six The Great Acceleration

1. T. H. Huxley, "Inaugural Address" at the London Fisheries Exhibition of 1883, http://aleph0.clarku.edu/huxley/SM5/fish.html.

2. F. Berkes et al., "Globalization, Roving Bandits, and Marine Resources," *Science* 311 (2006): 1557–58.

3. On the development of the conservation movement see Samuel P. Hays, *Conservation and the Gospel of Efficiency: The Progressive Conservation Movement, 1890–1920* (New York: Atheneum, 1975).

4. See W. Steffen et al., *Global Change and the Earth System: A Planet Under Pressure* (Berlin: Springer Verlag, 2004). On the development of the concept of the Anthropocene see Will Steffen, Jacques Grinevald, Paul J. Crutzen, and John R. McNeill, "The Anthropocene: Conceptual and Historical Perspectives," *Philosophical Transactions of the Royal Society A* 369 (2011): 842–67. The concept has entered into general usage, as reflected in the cover story entitled, "Welcome to the Anthropocene," *Economist* 399, no. 8735 (May 28–June 3, 2011).

5. For the initial development of this now well-known formula see Paul R. Ehrlich and John P. Holdren, "Impact of Population Growth," *Science* 171 (1971): 1212–17.

6. On the concept of the Great Acceleration see Will Steffen, Paul J. Crutzen, and John R. McNeill, "The Anthropocene: Are Humans Now Overwhelming the Great Forces of Nature?" *Ambio* 36 (2007): 614–21.

7. B. L. Turner II et al., *The Earth as Transformed by Human Action: Global and Regional Changes in the Biosphere over the Past 300 Years* (Cambridge: Cambridge University Press, 1990); and John R. McNeill, *Something New Under the Sun: An Environmental History of the Twentieth-Century World* (New York: W. W. Norton, 2000).

8. See Jared Diamond, *Collapse: How Societies Choose to Fail or Succeed* (New York: Viking, 2005).

9. Mancur Olson Jr., *Power and Prosperity: Outgrowing Communist and Capitalist Dictatorships* (New York: Basic Books, 2000).

10. Christopher McGrory Klyza, *Who Controls Public Lands? Mining, Forestry, and Grazing Policies, 1870–1990* (Chapel Hill: University of North Carolina Press, 1996).

11. See Wallace Stegner, *Beyond the Hundredth Meridian: John Wesley Powell and the Second Opening of the West* (Boston: Houghton-Mifflin, 1954).

12. See Douglas G. Brinkley, *The Wilderness Warrior: Theodore Roosevelt and the Crusade for America* (New York: Harper, 2010).

13. Steffen et al., *Global Change and the Earth System.*

14. The basic figures are drawn from "World Population," Wikipedia, http://en.wikipedia.org/wiki/world_population. But see also David E. Bloom, "7 Billion and Counting," *Science* 333 (2011): 562–69.

15. Hans Joachim Schellnhuber, Paul J. Crutzen, William C. Clark, and Julian Hunt, "Earth System Analysis for Sustainability," *Environment* 47 (October 2005): 12.

16. Ibid.

17. Peter M. Vitousek, Harold A. Mooney, Jane Lubchenco, and Jerry M. Melillo, "Human Domination of the Earth's Ecosystems," *Science* 277 (1997): 498.

18. Steffen et al., *Global Change and the Earth System.*

19. Steffen et al., "The Anthropocene," 614.

20. For an interesting effort to address the implications of this observation see George A. Akerlof and Rachel E. Kranton, *Identity Economics: How Our Identities Shape Our Work, Wages, and Well-Being* (Princeton, NJ: Princeton University Press, 2011).

21. See Kari Norgaard, *Living in Denial: Climate Change, Emotions, and Everyday Life* (Cambridge, MA: MIT Press, 2011).

22. Oran R. Young et al., "The Globalization of Socio-Ecological Systems: An Agenda for Scientific Research," *Global Environmental Change* 16 (2006): 304–16.

23. See M. H. Glantz, R. W. Katz, and N. Nicholls, *Teleconnections Linking Worldwide Climate Anomalies: Scientific Basis and Societal Impact* (Cambridge: Cambridge University Press, 1991).

24. Timothy M. Lenton et al., "Tipping Elements in the Earth's Climate System," *Proceedings of the National Academy of Sciences* 105 (2008): 1786.

25. Johan Rockström et al., "A Safe Operating Space for Humanity," *Nature* 461 (2009): 472–75.

26. Robert W. Kates, Thomas M. Parris, and Anthony A. Leiserowitz, "What Is Sustainable Development? Goals, Indicators, Values, and Practice," *Environment* 47 (April 2005): 8–21.

27. United Nations Millennium Declaration, UN General Assembly, Res. 55/2, http://www.un.org/millennium/declaration/areas552e.htm.

28. Frank Biermann, "Earth System Governance as a Crosscutting Theme of Global Change Research," *Global Environmental Change* 17 (2007): 326–37.

Chapter Seven The Sustainability Transition

1. On this theme see the Earth System Governance Project, http://www.earthsystemgovernance.org/.

2. See Oran R. Young, "Navigating the Sustainability Transition: Governing Complex and Dynamic Socioecological Systems," in Eric Brousseau et al., eds., *Global Environmental Commons: Analytical and Political Challenges in Building Governance Mechanisms* (Oxford: Oxford University Press, forthcoming).

3. See Robert W. Kates and Thomas M. Parris, "Science and Technology for Sustainable Development: Long-Term Trends and a Sustainability Transition," *Proceedings of the National Academy of Sciences* 100 (2003): 8062–67.

4. T. H. Huxley, "Inaugural Address" at the London Fisheries Exhibition of 1883, http://aleph0.Clarku.edu/Huxley/SM5/fish.html.

5. For an introduction to the concept of self-fulfilling prophecy see "Self-Fulfilling Prophecy," Wikipedia, http://en.wikipedia.org/wiki/Self-fulfilling_prophecy.

6. See Oran R. Young et al., "The Globalization of Socio-Ecological Systems: An Agenda for Scientific Research," *Global Environmental Change* 16 (2006): 304–16.

7. Kari Norgaard, *Living in Denial: Climate Change, Emotions, and Everyday Life* (Cambridge, MA: MIT Press, 2011).

8. For a range of perspectives on adaptation to climate change see W. Neil Adger, Irene Lorenzoni, and Karen O'Brien, eds., *Adapting to Climate Change: Thresholds, Values, and Governance* (Cambridge: Cambridge University Press, 2009).

9. In the 2009 Copenhagen Accord the UNFCCC Annex 1 countries promised to make available $30 billion for climate mitigation and adaptation during 2010–2012 and to ramp up this amount to $100 billion per year by 2020. The text of the accord can be found at http://unfccc.int.

10. See Peter Bachrach and Morton S. Baratz, "Decisions and Nondecisions: An Analytical Framework," *American Political Science Review* 57 (1963): 632–42.

11. Johan Rockström et al., "A Safe Operating Space for Humanity," *Nature* 461 (2009): 472–75.

12. Amos Tversky and Daniel Kahneman, "Judgment Under Uncertainty: Heuristics and Biases," *Science* 185 (1974): 1124–31.

13. See Leila Sievanen et al., "Linking Top-Down and Bottom-Up Processes through the New U.S. National Ocean Policy," *Conservation Letters*, forthcoming.

14. James G. March and Johan P. Olsen, "The Institutional Dynamics of International Political Orders," *International Organization* 52 (1998): 943–69.

15. For a suggestive effort to address this issue see George A. Akerlof and Rachel E. Kranton, *Identity Economics: How Our Identities Shape Our Work, Wages, and Well-Being* (Princeton, NJ: Princeton University Press, 2011).

16. See Steven G. Calabresi and Lucy D. Bickford, "Federalism and Subsidiarity: Perspectives from Law," paper delivered at the 2011 annual meeting of the American Society of Political and Legal Philosophy.

17. See Edward A. Parson, *Protecting the Ozone Layer: Science and Strategy* (New York: Oxford University Press, 2003).

18. On recent efforts under the auspices of the Convention on Biological Diversity to work toward increasing the size of protected areas see the decisions of COP 10 in 2010, http://www.cbd.int.

19. For a variety of perspectives on this issue see Frank Biermann and Stefan Bauer, eds., *A World Environment Organization: Solution or Threat for Effective International Environmental Governance?* (Aldershot, UK: Ashgate, 2005).

20. For background on the origins of the GATT see Kenneth Dam, *The GATT: Law and International Economic Organization* (Chicago: University of Chicago Press, 1970).

21. The text of the UN Millennium Declaration, adopted as UN General Assembly Res. 55/2 on September 8, 2000, is available at http://www.un.org/millennium/declaration/ares552e.htm.

22. See John W. Kingdon, *Agendas, Alternatives, and Public Policies*, 2nd ed. (New York: Harper Collins, 1995).

23. On the issue of environmental refugees see Frank Biermann and Ingrid Boas, "Protecting Climate Refugees: The Case for a Global Protocol," *Environment* 50 (November 2008): 8–16.

24. On recent thinking regarding the concept of a green economy see UNEP, *Towards a Green Economy: Pathways to Sustainable Development and Poverty Eradication*, 2011, http://www.unep.org/green economy.

25. For a range of perspectives on geopolitics see Gearoid Tuathail, Simon Dalby, and Paul Routledge, *The Geopolitics Reader* (London: Routledge, 2006).

26. Magali A. Delmas and Oran R. Young, eds., *Governance for the Environment: New Perspectives* (Cambridge: Cambridge University Press, 2009).

27. See Klaus Dingwerth, *The New Transnationalism: Transnational Governance and Democratic Legitimacy* (New York: Palgrave Macmillan, 2007), and Philipp Pattberg, *Private Institutions and Global Governance: The New Ethics of Environmental Sustainability* (Cheltenham, UK: Edward Elgar, 2007).

28. See Maria Carmen Lemos and Arun Agrawal, "Environmental Governance in Political Science," in Magali A. Delmas and Oran R. Young, eds., *Governance for the Environment: New Perspectives*, 69–97 (Cambridge: Cambridge University Press, 2009).

29. This quote is from the Stockholm Memorandum issued at the 3rd Nobel Laureate Symposium on Global Sustainability, May 18, 2011, text available at http://www.globalsymposium2011.org.

Conclusion: Making Environmental Governance Work

1. For a discussion of the generalizability of propositions about human-environment relations across issue domains see Oran R. Young, ed., *Global Governance: Drawing Insights from the Environmental Experience* (Cambridge, MA: MIT Press, 1997).

2. See Oran R. Young, *The Institutional Dimensions of Environmental Change: Fit, Interplay, and Scale* (Cambridge, MA: MIT Press, 2002), ch. 7; Elinor Ostrom, "A Diagnostic Approach for Going Beyond Panaceas," *Proceedings of the National Academy of Sciences* 104 (September 25, 2007):

15181–187; and Oran R. Young, "Building Regimes for Socioecological Systems: Institutional Diagnostics," in Oran R. Young, Leslie A. King, and Heike Schroeder, eds., *Institutions and Environmental Change*, 115–44 (Cambridge, MA: MIT Press, 2008).

3. James G. March and Johan P. Olsen, *Rediscovering Institutions: The Organizational Basis of Politics* (New York: The Free Press, 1989).

4. For a discussion of this point based on the distinction between coordination problems and collaboration problems see Arthur Stein, "Coordination and Collaboration Regimes in an Anarchic World," *International Organization* 36 (1982): 299–324.

5. Oran R. Young, "Navigating the Sustainability Transition," in Eric Brousseau et al., eds., *Global Environmental Commons: Analytical and Political Challenges in Building Governance Mechanisms* (Oxford: Oxford University Press, forthcoming).

6. For a thoughtful discussion using the concepts of benign and malign problems see Edward L. Miles, Arild Underdal, Steinar Andresen, Jørgen Wettestad, Jon Birger Skjaerseth, and Elaine M. Carlin, *Environmental Regime Effectiveness: Confronting Theory with Evidence* (Cambridge, MA: MIT Press, 2002).

7. See, for example, Will Steffen, "Climate Change: A Truly Complex and Diabolical Policy Problem," in John Dryzek, Richard Norgaard, and David Schlosberg, eds., *Oxford Handbook of Climate Change and Society*, 21–37 (Oxford: Oxford University Press, 2011).

8. On the distinction between systemic and cumulative problems see B. L. Turner II et al., "Two Types of Global Environmental Change: Definitional and Spatial Scale Issues in Their Human Dimensions," *Global Environmental Change* 1 (1991): 14–22.

9. On the nature of regime complexes see Kal Raustiala and David G. Victor, "The Regime Complex for Plant Genetic Resources," *International Organization* 55 (2004): 277–309, and Robert O. Keohane and David G. Victor, "The Regime Complex for Climate," *Perspectives on Politics* 9 (2011): 7–23.

10. See UNEP, *Toward a Green Economy: Pathways to Sustainable Development and Poverty Eradication—A Synthesis for Policymakers*, 2011, www.unep.org/greeneconomy.

11. Aldo Leopold, "The Land Ethic," in Aldo Leopold, *A Sand County Almanac with Essays on Conservation from Round River*, 237–64 (New York: Ballantine Books, 1970).

12. On stewardship as a lens through which to look at human-environmental relations see F. Stewart Chapin III, Gary Kofinas, and

Carl Folke, eds., *Principles of Ecosystem Stewardship* (New York: Springer, 2009).

13. See Edward A. Parson, *Protecting the Ozone Layer: Science and Strategy* (New York: Oxford University Press, 2003).

14. See, for example, the debate between Nicholas Stern and his critics as exemplified in Nicholas Stern, *The Economics of Climate Change: The Stern Review* (Cambridge: Cambridge University Press, 2007); and William D. Nordhaus, "A Review of the Stern Review on the Economics of Climate Change," *Journal of Economic Literature* xlv (2007): 686–702.

15. Experience in other cases, such as the arrangements created to reduce emissions of ozone-depleting substances and of sulfur dioxide and nitrogen oxides, suggests that ex ante estimates of the costs of addressing such concerns often exceed the real costs of doing so by a wide margin.

16. For a general account of allocation issues see Leigh Raymond, *Private Property in Public Resources: Equity and Property Allocation in Market-Based Environmental Policy* (Washington, DC: Resources for the Future Press, 2003).

17. For general discussions of compliance with the terms of environmental regimes see Ronald B. Mitchell, "Compliance Theory: An Overview," in James Cameron, Jacob Werksman, and Peter Roderick, eds., *Improving Compliance with International Law*, 3–28 (London: Earthscan, 1996), and Kal Raustiala and Anne-Marie Slaughter, "International Law, International Relations and Compliance," in Walter Carlsnaes, Thomas Risse, and Beth A. Simmons, eds., *Handbook of International Relations*, 538–58 (London: Sage Publications, 2002).

18. See Rosalind Reeve, *Policing International Trade in Endangered Species: The CITES Treaty and Compliance* (London: Royal Institute of International Affairs and Earthscan, 2002).

19. For a range of perspectives on this issue, with particular emphasis on environmental governance in small-scale societies, see Elinor Ostrom et al., eds., *The Drama of the Commons* (Washington, DC: National Academy Press, 2002).

20. See Young, "Navigating the Sustainability Transition: Governing Complex and Dynamic Socioecological Systems."

21. See Timothy Lenton et al., "Tipping Elements in the Earth's Climate System," *Proceedings of the National Academy of Sciences* 105 (February 12, 2008): 1786–93.

22. For an overview framed in terms of the discourse of resilience and adaptation see Brian Walker and David Salt, *Resilience Thinking:*

Sustaining Ecosystems and People in a Changing World (Washington, DC: Island Press, 2006).

23. For the details of this case see Parson, *Protecting the Ozone Layer.*

24. On the implications of this proposition for institutional design see Young, "Building Regimes for Socioecological Systems."

Index

About the Author

Oran Young is a research professor and co-director of the Program on Governance for Sustainable Development at the Bren School of Environmental Science & Management at the University of California, Santa Barbara. His research focuses on theories of environmental governance with applications to issues relating to climate change, marine systems, and the polar regions. Dr. Young served for six years as founding chair of the Committee on the Human Dimensions of Global Change of the US National Academy of Sciences, and he chaired the Scientific Steering Committee of the international project on the Institutional Dimensions of Global Environmental Change (IDGEC). He was a founding co-chair of the Global Carbon Project and from 2005 to 2010 chaired the Scientific Committee of the International Human Dimensions Programme on Global Environmental Change. An expert on Arctic issues, Dr. Young recently chaired the Steering Committee of the Arctic Governance Project. Past service in this realm includes co-chair of the Working Group on Arctic International Relations, vice-president of the International Arctic Science Committee, chair of the Board of Governors of the University of the Arctic, consultant to the Standing Committee of Parliamentarians of the Arctic

Region, and co-chair of the 2004 Arctic Human Development Report. He is the author of more than twenty books. His recent books include *Institutional Dynamics: Emergent Patterns in International Environmental Governance* (2010) and (with others) *Science Diplomacy* (2011).